HOW TO
Win Chess Games Quickly

(Including 120 pages published under the
title, *How to Beat Your Opponent Quickly*)

FRED REINFELD

BARNES & NOBLE, INC.   New York
Publishers • Booksellers • Since 1873

An Everyday Handbook

Contents

A REVIEW FOR BEGINNERS

Perhaps you already know the elements of chess. If so, fine. If not, here's a quick summary of what you need to know about the game:

The game is played on a chessboard, with eight horizontal rows and eight vertical rows of eight squares each. All 64 squares are used.

Each player has 16 chessmen: one King, one Queen, two Rooks (or Castles), two Bishops, two Knights, and eight Pawns.

To see how these forces are placed, refer to the diagram on page 9. At the beginning of the game, the King is placed on K1. The Queen is placed on Q1. The Bishops are placed on KB1 and QB1. The Knights are placed on KN1 and QN1. The Rooks are placed on KR1 and QR1.

All the chessmen mentioned thus far go on the horizontal row nearest the player. The Pawns go on the next horizontal row—at KR2, KN2, KB2, K2, Q2, QB2, QN2, and QR2. When you are all through setting up the pieces, this is the position you will have for starting the game:

The following statements indicate how the chessmen move:

The King can move in any direction, one square at a time.

The Queen can move vertically, horizontally, and diagonally along the whole length of any line available to her. Friendly pieces may block her path, while enemy pieces on these lines can be captured by her.

The Rook can move horizontally and vertically—but only one direction at a time.

The Bishop moves diagonally, one direction at a time.

The Knight is the only piece that can leap over any other units. Its move is always of the same length: it moves one square up or down, and then two squares to the right or left. It can capture hostile pieces only at the terminal square of its move.

The King, Queen, Rook, Bishop, and Knight all capture the way they move.

The Pawn has some curious properties. It can only move forward, one square at a time. The first time it moves, it can advance two squares. In capturing, however, it captures diagonally forward on an adjoining square.

The most important power of the Pawn is that' when it reaches the last row, you can promote it to a new Queen, Rook, Bishop, or Knight. In almost all cases the new piece is a Queen—for this is the strongest of all the pieces.

Basically, the way to win a game of chess is to attack the hostile King in such a way that no matter what your opponent does, he cannot escape capture.

When the King is attacked, he is said to be in check. If he can get out of check, the game goes on. If he·cannot get out of check, the King is checkmated, and the game is over.

A prospective loser does not always wait for checkmate.

If he has lost too much material, he knows checkmate is inevitable, and so he resigns. If on the other hand there is not enough material to force checkmate, the game is given up as a draw, with honors even.

Here are a few more rules you need to know: White always moves first, and the board is so placed that the nearest corner square at his right is a white square. In order to get the King into a safe position, it is advisable to "castle." This is possible on the King-side when there are no pieces between the King and King Rook. Move the King next to the Rook, and then place the Rook on the other side of the King. It is also possible to castle with the Queen Rook when there are no pieces between the King and the Queen Rook. In that case, the King moves to QB1, and the Queen Rook goes to Q1.

To derive the maximum value of this book, there are two features that you will very likely want to review quickly. One is to check up on the relative values of the chessmen. Expressed in points, their values are as follows:

Queen	9 points
Rook	5 points
Bishop	3 points
Knight	3 points
Pawn	1 point

It is important to be absolutely certain of these values, for most games are decided by superiority in force.

Bishops (3 points) and Knights (3 points) are equal in value, but experienced players try to capture a Bishop in return for a Knight.

A Bishop or Knight (3 points) is worth about three Pawns (3 points). If you give up a Knight and get three

Pawns in return, you may consider it as more or less an even exchange. If you lose a Knight (3 points) for only a Pawn (1 point), you have lost material and should lose the game, if you are playing against an expert.

If you capture a Rook (5 points) for a Bishop or Knight (3 points), you are said to have "won the Exchange." If you lose a Rook (5 points) for a Bishop or Knight (3 points), you have "lost the Exchange."

The other important feature in reading a chess book is to be familiar with chess notation. If you can count up to 8, this presents no problem. You may have heard scare stories to the effect that chess notation is inordinately difficult. The difficulty of chess notation is a myth, circulated by people too lazy to discover how simple and logical it really is.

The following diagram shows you all you need to know about chess notation:

BLACK

QR1 / QR8	QN1 / QN8	QB1 / QB8	Q1 / Q8	K1 / K8	KB1 / KB8	KN1 / KN8	KR1 / KR8
QR2 / QR7	QN2 / QN7	QB2 / QB7	Q2 / Q7	K2 / K7	KB2 / KB7	KN2 / KN7	KR2 / KR7
QR3 / QR6	QN3 / QN6	QB3 / QB6	Q3 / Q6	K3 / K6	KB3 / KB6	KN3 / KN6	KR3 / KR6
QR4 / QR5	QN4 / QN5	QB4 / QB5	Q4 / Q5	K4 / K5	KB4 / KB5	KN4 / KN5	KR4 / KR5
QR5 / QR4	QN5 / QN4	QB5 / QB4	Q5 / Q4	K5 / K4	KB5 / KB4	KN5 / KN4	KR5 / KR4
QR6 / QR3	QN6 / QN3	QB6 / QB3	Q6 / Q3	K6 / K3	KB6 / KB3	KN6 / KN3	KR6 / KR3
QR7 / QR2	QN7 / QN2	QB7 / QB2	Q7 / Q2	K7 / K2	KB7 / KB2	KN7 / KN2	KR7 / KR2
QR8 / QR1	QN8 / QN1	QB8 / QB1	Q8 / Q1	K8 / K1	KB8 / KB1	KN8 / KN1	KR8 / KR1

WHITE

As you see, the squares are *numbered* from both sides of the board; White's KR1, for example, is Black's KR8. Each square is also *named* for the piece occupying the file.

I honestly believe that *ten minutes' study* of this board is all you need to enable you to play over the games and examples in this book.* Although the compact treatment of games and examples makes only slight demands on your knowledge of chess notation, I should like to advise you to master the notation thoroughly; it will open the gates to a lifetime of reading pleasure.

The following are the chief abbreviations used in the chess notation:

King	— K	discovered check	— dis ch
Queen	— Q	double check	— dbl ch
Rook	— R	en passant	— e.p.
Bishop	— B	castles, king-side	— O—O
Knight	— N	castles, queen-side	— O—O—O
Pawn	— P	good move	— !
captures	— x	very good move	— ! !
to	— —	outstanding move	— ! ! !
check	— ch	bad move	— ?

Here are some examples of abbreviation: N—KB3 means "Knight moves to King Bishop three." Q x B means "Queen takes Bishop." R—K8ch means "Rook moves to King eight giving check."

---

* For a detailed treatment of chess notation, see *First Book of Chess* (New York: Barnes & Noble, Inc., 1954) by I. Horowitz and F. Reinfeld.

NOTE TO THE READER

We all want to win, and if we can win quickly, so much the better. But here is a queer paradox: it's sometimes easier to win quickly than to win in a long, hard, tiring fight.

The reason? Simple enough. When we look at the score of a game that went 60 or 70 moves or more, we take for granted that it was hard fought, or else that very few opportunities were available to either player. But these assumptions are often wrong! In the games between ordinary players, priceless opportunities are missed constantly. Especially is this true in the very *opening* stage. So my thesis is, win quickly—and save yourself a lot of trouble.

Winning quickly — that's easier said than done, you may think. Actually, there are definite landmarks in a game that help you to see a decisive advantage. When your opponent's King is exposed to attack; when he has neglected his development; when his Queen is out of play; when he has overlooked an important tactical point—these are the situations in which you can win quickly—in as few as five moves!

If you're skeptical, turn the page, start reading—and see for yourself.

1. How to Win When Your Opponent's King Is Exposed to Attack

Very often—far more frequently than you realize—the opportunity presents itself to attack a hostile King stranded in the center. This King is caught in the crossfire of your own actively posted pieces. Go after him, force checkmate, or gain decisive material.

The types of positions you will encounter can be divided into four different kinds. First there are the "King Hunts" (pages 13-18), where your opponent's King has been so badly compromised that you can hound him over the board to his doom.

Then there are the games in which your opponent has weakened his position irretrievably by some Pawn move (pages 20-26). Such inconspicuous little moves often give you your big chance.

Your opponents go wrong more often than you think, by plunging into complications without adequately safeguarding their King. The games on pages 27-32 show you how to take advantage of that mistake.

Sometimes your opponents make thoughtless moves quite early in the opening which expose their King to disaster. The games on pages 33-35 are good examples.

Study each of these brief, convincing games until you're sure you can apply the winning procedure yourself.

PHILIDOR'S DEFENSE

Black's mistake: Black opens up the game prematurely with
3 . . . P—KB4?? (instead of the safe developing move 3 . . .
N—KB3!).

White's refutation: Realizing that Black's King is fatally
exposed to attack, White thrusts powerfully at the center
(4 P—Q4!) and then hits out at the weak spot King Bishop
7 with 7 N—KN5!

	WHITE	BLACK
1	P—K4	P—K4
2	N—KB3	P—Q3
3	B—B4	P—KB4??

Enormously extending the range of White's King Bishop.

	WHITE	BLACK
4	P—Q4!	N—KB3
5	N—B3	KPxP
6	QxP	B—Q2
7	N—KN5!	N—B3

(Position after 7 . . . N—B3)

Thanks to Black's mistaken policy of exposing his King to attack, White can now execute a forced checkmate in five moves!

| 8 | B—B7ch | K—K2 |
| 9 | QxNch!! | KxQ |

Or 9 . . . PxQ; 10 N—Q5 mate.

10	N—Q5ch	K—K4
11	N—B3ch	KxP
12	N—B3 mate	

KING'S GAMBIT

Black's mistakes: Black grabs too many Pawns and loses priceless time with 8 . . . B—N6?? (instead of 8 . . . P—Q4!; 9 BxP, N—KB3!).

White's refutation: Relying on his superior development, White sacrifices piece after piece for a brilliant mate.

WHITE		BLACK
1	P—K4	P—K4
2	N—QB3	P—Q3
3	P—B4	PxP
4	N—B3	B—K2
5	B—B4	B—R5ch
6	P—KN3	PxP
7	Castles	PxPch
8	K—R1	B—N6??

9	BxPch!	KxB
10	N—K5 dbl ch	K—K3
11	Q—N4ch!	KxN
12	P—Q4ch!	KxQP
13	B—K3ch!	KxB
14	QR—Q1!!	. . .

(Position after 14 QR—Q1!!)

White threatens no less than six different check-mates! Naturally Black cannot parry all the threats.

14	. . .	BxQ
15	R—Q3 mate	

SICILIAN DEFENSE

Black's mistakes: All of Black's first six moves are Pawn moves—with not a piece developed!

White's refutation: With three pieces in action, White hacks away at the unprotected Black King and drives him into a mating net.

WHITE	BLACK
1 P—K4	P—QB4
2 P—Q4	PxP
3 N—KB3	P—K4?
4 P—B3	PxP
5 NxBP	P—Q3
6 B—QB4	P—KR3?

(Position after 6 . . . P—KR3?)

With his tremendous lead in development, White can sacrifice material right and left to force an amusing checkmate.

7 BxPch!	KxB
8 NxPch	K—K2
9 N—Q5ch	K—K3
10 Q—N4ch!	KxN
11 B—KB4ch	K—Q5
12 B—K3ch!	K—K4

If 12 . . . K—B5; 13 Q—K2 mate.

13 Q—B4ch	K—K3
14 Q—B5 mate	

KING KNIGHT OPENING

Black's mistakes: Black chooses the constricting 3 . . . P—Q3? (instead of 3 . . . B—B4!) and repeats the error with 4 . . . KN—K2? (instead of 4 . . . N—B3!).

White's refutation: White starts an immediate attack to exploit Black's inferior development.

WHITE	BLACK
1 P—K4	P—K4
2 N—KB3	N—QB3
3 B—B4	P—Q3?
4 Castles	KN—K2?
5 N—N5	P—B3
6 B—B7ch	K—Q2
7 Q—N4ch	P—B4
8 PxP	P—KR4

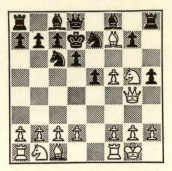

(Position after 8 . . . P—KR4)

White was threatening mate beginning with P—B6 dis ch. Black hopes to meet the threat by attacking White's Queen. However, Black's King is so badly exposed that White can sacrifice his Queen to get a ferocious discovered check.

9	P—B6 dis ch!!	PxQ
10	B—K6ch	K—K1
11	P—B7 mate	

RUY LOPEZ

Black's mistakes: Black's faulty 6 . . . NxQP? allows White to subject the Black King to attack. The result is that the King becomes a target.

White's refutation: White's agile Queen works wonders. A notable finesse is 13 NxN!! instead of the more obvious 13 P—B3 to regain the piece.

WHITE	BLACK
1 P—K4	P—K4
2 N—KB3	N—QB3
3 B—N5	P—QR3
4 B—R4	N—B3
5 P—Q4	P—QN4
6 B—N3	NxQP?
7 BxPch!	KxB
8 NxPch	K—K3
9 QxN	P—B4
10 Q—B3	NxP
11 Q—K3	KxN
12 N—B3!	P—Q4
13 NxN!!	....

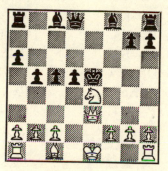

(Position after 13 NxN!!)

Now the beauty and subtlety of White's ingenious plan is revealed. On 13 ... PxN; 14 Q—B4ch!, K—K3; 15 QxPch picks up Black's Queen Rook. Black avoids this but soon resigns in despair, as the position of his King is hopeless.

19

13 ...	P—Q5
14 Q—KB3	B—Q2
15 Castles	B—K2
16 R—K1	Resigns

RUY LOPEZ

Black's mistakes: After an early . . . P—B4 Black's un-castled King is soon exposed to attack. Black's further heedless play gives White his chance.

White's refutation: Concentrating on the exposed position of Black's King, White sacrifices pieces unstintingly.

WHITE	BLACK
1 P—K4	P—K4
2 N—KB3	N—QB3
3 B—N5	P—B4
4 N—B3	PxP
5 QNxP	N—B3
6 NxNch	PxN
7 P—Q4!	P—K5

(Position after 7 . . . P—K5)

White now offers a piece with 8 N—N5! He sees that after 8 . . . PxN; 9 Q—R5ch, K—K2 he wins the Black Queen with 10 BxPch.

8	N—N5!	B—N5ch
9	P—B3	PxN
10	Q—R5ch	K—B1
11	BxP	N—K2

Or 11 . . . B—K2; 12 B—KR6ch, K—N1; 13 B—QB4ch, P—Q4; 14 BxPch, QxB; 15 Q—K8ch followed by mate.

12	B—QB4	P—Q4
13	BxP!	Resigns

For if 13 . . . QxB; 14 B—R6ch, K—N1; 15 Q—K8 mate.

FRENCH DEFENSE

Black's mistake: Nothing can weaken your position like an ill-judged Pawn move. Thus Black's 8 . . . P—QB3?? (instead of 8 . . . P—QR3) opens the gates to the enemy.

White's refutation: After gaining an entry with 9 N—Q6ch, White forces the pace vigorously by bringing new forces to the attack. This makes a brilliant finish possible.

	WHITE	BLACK
1	P—K4	P—K3
2	P—Q4	P—Q4
3	N—QB3	N—KB3

4	B—KN5	B—K2
5	P—K5	KN—Q2
6	BxB	QxB
7	N—N5	Q—Q1
8	B—Q3	P—QB3??
9	N—Q6ch	K—K2
10	Q—R5	P—KN3
11	Q—R4ch	P—B3
12	N—R3!	N—R3
13	N—KB4	P—KN4

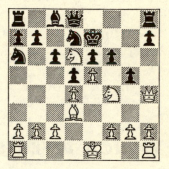

(Position after 13 . . . P—KN4)

Black expects to win a piece, but he is sadly mistaken. White has seen further ahead, and has prepared a stunning refutation.

14	QxRPch!!	RxQ
15	N—N6 mate	

BISHOP'S OPENING

Black's mistakes: Black plays the opening too passively (3 . . . B—K2? instead of 3 . . . P—B3 followed by 4 . . . P—Q4). Again 4 . . . PxP? leads to an intolerably congested position in which a normal development is no longer possible for Black.

White's refutation: White develops rapidly, quickly centralizing his Queen for a vicious double attack.

	WHITE	BLACK
1	P—K4	P—K4
2	B—B4	N—KB3
3	P—Q3	B—K2?
4	P—B4!	PxP?
5	P—K5!	N—N1
6	N—QB3	P—Q3
7	QBxP	PxP
8	Q—R5!	. . .

For if 8 . . . PxB; 9 QxBPch, K—Q2; 10 B—K6ch, K—B3; 11 BxB, QxB; 12 Q—Q5ch, K—N3; 13 Q—QN5 mate.

8	. . .	P—KN3
9	QxKP	N—KB3
10	N—Q5!	QN—Q2
11	NxPch	Resigns

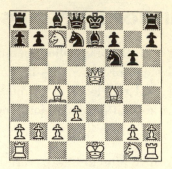

(Position after 11 NxPch)

White wins the Queen or forces checkmate, for example 11 . . . K—B1; 12 B—KR6ch, K—N1; 13 BxPch!, KxB; 14 Q—K6 mate.

MAX LANGE ATTACK

Black's mistakes: By losing the castling privilege early in the game, Black exposes his King to attack. His 12 . . . B—N3? (instead of 12 . . . B—KB1) deprives his King of needed protection.

White's refutation: White concentrates his forces against the exposed King. He carries through a successful assault by means of a startling sacrifice.

WHITE	BLACK
1 P—K4	P—K4
2 N—KB3	N—QB3
3 B—B4	B—B4

4 Castles	N—B3
5 P—Q4	PxP
6 P—K5	P—Q4
7 PxN	PxB
8 R—K1ch	K—B1?
9 B—N5!	PxP
10 B—R6ch	K—N1
11 N—B3!	B—KN5
12 N—K4	B—N3?
13 Q—K2!	. . .

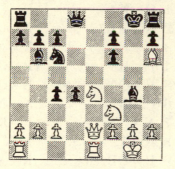

(Position after 13 Q—K2!)

White's attack against the exposed Black King is well organized. His immediate threat is 14 NxPch!, QxN; 15 Q—K8ch!, RxQ; 16 RxR mate. Thus he exacts the full punishment for Black's faulty 12 ... B—N3?

13 ...	N—K4
14 NxN!!!	BxQ
15 N—Q7!!!	Resigns

White forces checkmate by 16 NxPch!

25

RUY LOPEZ

Black's mistakes: Black's development becomes too congested after the ultra-passive 3 . . . KN—K2? (instead of 3 . . . N—KB3). And 7 . . . P—KR3? loses valuable time; it also weakens the support of Black's King Knight.

White's refutation: Relying on his far more aggressive development, White sacrifices a piece for a decisive attack.

WHITE	BLACK
1 P—K4	P—K4
2 N—KB3	N—QB3
3 B—N5	KN—K2?
4 P—B3	P—Q3
5 P—Q4	B—Q2
6 Castles	N—N3
7 N—N5	P—KR3?
8 NxP!!	KxN
9 B—QB4ch	K—K2
10 Q—R5	Q—K1

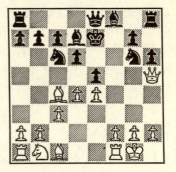

(Position after 10 . . . Q—K1)

Though White has fewer pieces in play than Black, what matters is that White has the initiative and that Black's King is badly exposed. In fact, White is on the point of bringing off a spectacular checkmate.

If 10 . . . B—K1; 11 B—KN5ch!, PxB; 12 QxPch, K—Q2; 13 Q—B5ch, K—K2; 14 Q—K6 mate.

KING'S GAMBIT

White's mistake: White decides on complications before assuring the safety of his own King. The combination of 6 B—B4 (instead of 6 P—Q4) and 7 NxP is particularly bad, as it allows the powerful reply 7 . . . Q—R5ch.

Black's refutation: Black starts a precisely timed counter-attack which fully exploits the exposed state of White's King.

	WHITE	BLACK
1	P—K4	P—K4
2	P—KB4	PxP
3	N—KB3	N—KB3
4	P—K5	N—R4
5	N—B3	P—Q3
6	B—B4	PxP
7	NxP	Q—R5ch
8	K—B1	B—K3!!
9	BxB	N—N6ch
10	K—N1	. . .

If instead 10 PxN, QxRch and Black has won the Exchange.

(Position after 10 K—N1)

Black now executes his grand combination. Note that his beautiful twelfth move is made possible by the enticing of White's Bishop from its diagonal at move 8.

10 . . .	B—B4ch!!
11 P—Q4	BxPch!!
12 QxB	N—K7ch!!
13 NxN	Q—K8 mate

SICILIAN DEFENSE

Black's mistake: One careless move condemns Black to disaster. 6 . . . NxN?? is immediately ruinous, whereas the careful retreat 6 . . . N—KB3 would protect his King adequately.

White's refutation: Where most players would despairingly resign themselves to the loss of a piece at move 7, White alertly seizes on the surprising 7 Q—B3!! as a move that leaves Black without any defense.

WHITE	BLACK
1 P—K4	P—QB4
2 N—KB3	N—KB3
3 N—B3	P—Q4
4 PxP	NxP
5 B—N5ch	B—Q2
6 N—K5!	NxN??

(Position after 6 . . . NxN??)

Black's last move seems conclusive, as he wins a piece after 7 NPxN? or 7 QPxN? or 7 BxBch?, NxB. Yet White has a move that forces Black's resignation in a few more moves!

7 Q—B3!!	P—B3
8 Q—R5ch	P—KN3
9 NxNP	K—B2
10 N—K5 dbl ch!	Resigns

If 10 . . . K—N2; 11 Q—B7ch, K—R3; 12 QPxN dis ch and mate!

Or 10 . . . K—K3; 11 B—B4ch and Black loses his Queen after 11 . . . K—Q3; 12 N—B7ch or 11 . . . N—Q4; 12 BxNch, KxB; 13 N—B7 dis ch.

BUDAPEST DEFENSE

White's mistakes: White loses valuable time recovering his Pawn because he plays 3 B—N5? (instead of the straightforward 3 PxP!).

Black's refutation: Black sets a sly trap based on the fact that White hasn't had time to complete his development and castle into safety.

	WHITE	BLACK
1	P—Q4	N—KB3
2	P—QB4	P—K4
3	B—N5?	PxP
4	N—KB3	B—N5ch
5	QN—Q2	N—B3
6	P—QR3	B—K2
7	N—N3	Castles
8	QNxP	P—Q4
9	P—K3	B—KN5
10	Q—B2	BxN
11	NxB	R—K1!
12	R—Q1	P—Q5!
13	NxP??	NxN
14	RxN	. . .

(Position after 14 RxN)

Black's Pawn sacrifice would be pointless if White's King were safely castled. But White's King is in the center, hence Black's combination works brilliantly. A sinister double check does the trick.

14 ...	QxR!!
15 PxQ	B—N5 dbl ch
16 K—Q1	R—K8 mate

BISHOP'S OPENING

Black's mistakes: Instead of developing his pieces effectively and castling promptly, Black embarks on a pathetically inadequate attack.

White's refutation: White develops his pieces very quickly and wins by an unusually elegant mating attack.

WHITE	BLACK
1 P—K4	P—K4
2 B—B4	N—KB3

3	N—KB3	NxP
4	N—B3	NxBP?
5	KxN	B—B4ch
6	P—Q4	PxP
7	R—K1ch	K—B1
8	N—K4	B—N3
9	Q—Q3!	P—Q4
10	Q—R3ch!	K—N1

(Position after 10 . . . K—N1)

Black is complacently under the impression that he is about to regain the piece. However, this is all part of White's subtle plan.

11	BxP!	QxB
12	N—B6ch!!	PxN
13	Q—B8ch!!	KxQ
14	B—R6ch	K—N1
15	R—K8 mate	

FRENCH DEFENSE

Black's mistakes: Black loses time with 5 . . . PxP (instead of the developing move 5 . . . N—K2!). His 7 . . . B—N3? (instead of the alert 7 . . . P—QR3!) allows the powerful 9 N—Q6ch later on.

White's refutation: Taking advantage of his opportunities, White builds up a mating attack.

	WHITE	BLACK
1	P—K4	P—K3
2	P—Q4	P—Q4
3	N—QB3	B—N5
4	P—K5	P—QB4
5	B—Q2	PxP
6	N—N5	B—B4
7	P—QN4	B—N3?
8	Q—N4	P—N3
9	N—Q6ch!	K—B1
10	Q—B4!	P—B3
11	PxP	B—B2

(Position after 11 . . . B—B2)

If instead 11 . . . P—KR4; 12 P—B7, N—R3; 13 QxNch!, RxQ; 14 BxRch, K—K2; 15 P—B8/Qch winning easily.

Completely oblivious of the threat, Black thinks he can win a piece. However, as the above variation shows, even on 11 . . . P—KR4 White could still have sacrificed his Queen.

12 Q—R6ch!!	NxQ
13 BxNch	K—N1
14 P—B7 mate	

RUY LOPEZ

Black's mistakes: After playing an opening variation which gives him a cramped game, Black should complete his development with 9 . . . B—K2 and 10 . . . Castles. (If then 10 NxRP?, P—B3 when the Knight is trapped.) Instead, he plays the careless 9 . . . Q—Q2?

White's refutation: With his more aggressive development, White can menace the uncastled Black King.

WHITE	BLACK
1 P—K4	P—K4
2 N—KB3	N—QB3
3 B—N5	N—B3
4 Castles	P—Q3
5 P—Q4	B—Q2
6 N—B3	PxP
7 NxP	NxN

8 QxN	BxB
9 NxB	Q—Q2?
10 P—K5!	P—B4

Either 10 . . . QxN; 11 PxN or 10 . . . PxP; 11 QxKPch is very unsatisfactory for Black.

11 Q—QR4!	...

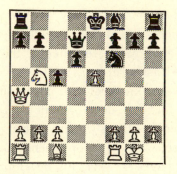

(Position after 11 Q—QR4!)

White threatens 12 PxN and also 12 N—B7ch! Black hopes to defend himself with 11 . . . N—Q4, although in that case 12 R—Q1 is decisive, for if 12 . . . Q—B3; 13 RxN!, QxR; 14 N—B7 dbl ch wins.

11 . . .	N—Q4
12 R—Q1	P—QR3
13 NxPch!	Resigns

For if 13 . . . BxN; 14 QxQch, KxQ; 15 RxN wins.

2. How to Win When Your Opponent Develops His Pieces Badly

Always be on the lookout for opportunities to take advantage of bad development by your opponent. When he brings out his pieces too slowly, or puts them on bad squares, or moves the same piece repeatedly, the chances are that you have some drastic reply available.

There are several kinds of bad development. There is, for example, self-blocking development (pages 37-40). This leads to congested positions which you can exploit vigorously.

And, of course, when your opponent moves the same piece twice or more (pages 41-48), his development is slowed up so grievously that you can make your own superior development tell quickly in your favor.

Sometimes you'll find that your opponent is developing his pieces fairly rapidly but ineptly—putting them on squares where they're ineffective (pages 50-54). A related fault is bad timing by your opponent—when he puts the right piece on the right square at the wrong time (pages 56-57). In either case you can often decide the game swiftly by a powerful attack.

In some cases you'll note your opponent making Pawn moves that are harmful or just a waste of time (pages 59-60). Here, too, you'll find glorious opportunities to punish your opponent for botching his development.

FOUR KNIGHTS' GAME

White's mistakes: White loses valuable time with his repeated Knight moves, beginning with 6 NxP. His 7 N—Q3? is particularly bad because it blocks the development of his Queen Bishop.

Black's refutation: Taking advantage of White's limited and ineffectual development, Black carries out a powerful attack based on superb development.

	WHITE	BLACK
1	P—K4	P—K4
2	N—KB3	N—QB3
3	N—B3	N—B3
4	B—N5	N—Q5
5	B—B4	B—B4
6	NxP	Q—K2
7	N—Q3?	P—Q4!
8	NxP	QxPch
9	N—K3	B—Q3
10	Castles	P—QN4!
11	B—N3	B—N2
12	N—K1	Q—R5!

With 12 ... Q—R5! Black forced the weakening advance of one of White's King-side Pawns. With 14 ... P—KR4! Black indicates that he will use White's King Knight Pawn as a target to open the King Rook file.

13 P—N3		Q—R6	
14 P—QB3		P—KR4!	

(Position after 14 . . . P—KR4)

15 PxN		P—R5!	
16 Q—K2		QxRPch!!	

White resigns, for if 17 KxQ, PxP dbl ch; 18 K—N1, R—R8 mate.

FOUR KNIGHTS' GAME

White's mistakes: As in the previous game, White loses time with 5 NxP and then blocks his development with 7 N—Q3? Later on, the frivolous 11 NxQP?? proves a fatal loss of time.

Black's refutation: Black develops rapidly and consistently with a view to a decisive onslaught on the King-side.

38

	WHITE	BLACK
1	P—K4	P—K4
2	N—KB3	N—QB3
3	N—B3	N—B3
4	B—N5	N—Q5
5	NxP	B—B4
6	B—R4	Castles
7	N—Q3?	B—N3
8	Castles	P—Q4
9	P—K5	N—K5
10	K—R1	Q—R5!
11	NxQP??	B—N5
12	Q—K1	. . .

If 12 P—KB3, N—KN6ch; 13 K—N1, NxKBP mate or
13 . . . N/Q5—K7.

12 . . .   N—KB6!

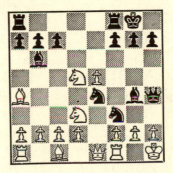

(Position after 12 . . . N—KB6!)

White resigns, for if 13 PxN, QBxPch; 14
K—N1, Q—N5 mate. The final position shows the

cumulative effect of Black's steady concentration of force on the King-side.

RUY LOPEZ

Black's mistake: By playing 7 . . . B—Q3?? (instead of 7 . . . B—N3) Black blocks his Queen Pawn, which in turn prevents the development of his Queen Bishop.

White's refutation: White utilizes his superior development to work up a devastating King-side attack.

WHITE	BLACK
1 P—K4	P—K4
2 N—KB3	N—QB3
3 B—N5	B—B4
4 P—B3	N—B3
5 P—Q3	Q—K2
6 Castles	Castles
7 P—Q4	B—Q3??
8 R—K1	N—K1
9 QN—Q2	N—Q1
10 N—B1	P—KB3
11 B—B4ch	N—B2
12 N—N3	P—KN3

Very weakening, as will be seen, but he cannot allow N—B5. Thus he pays the price for the inactivity of his Queen Bishop.

13 B—KR6	N—N2
14 N—R4!	PxP

| 15 Q—N4! | BxN |
| 16 NxP!! | Resigns |

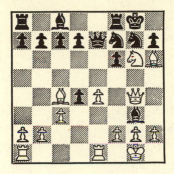

(Position after 16 NxP!!)

White has a forced win. If 16 . . . PxN; 17 QxNP followed by 18 QxN/N7 mate. Or if 16 . . . Q—K1; 17 N—K7ch! and mate next move. White exploited his opponent's lack of development in admirable style.

CARO-KANN DEFENSE

Black's mistakes: The ineffectual and time-wasting development of Black's Knights is enough to cost the game. Another unfortunate idea is 6 . . . P—KN3?, for after 8 . . . P—K3 the square King Bishop 3 is very weak.

White's refutation: With 8 N—K5! White forces a serious weakness at Black's King Bishop 3. With 11 B—KN5! White sets up a powerful pin.

WHITE	BLACK
1 P—K4	P—QB3
2 N—QB3	P—Q4
3 N—B3	PxP
4 NxP	N—Q2
5 P—Q4	QN—B3?
6 N—B5	P—KN3?
7 B—QB4	N—R3?
8 N—K5!	P—K3
9 Q—B3	N—B4
10 P—B3	B—N2
11 B—KN5!	Castles
12 N—K4!	P—KR4

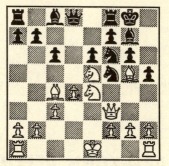

(Position after 12 . . . P—KR4)

Black's last move was played to stop N—N4, which would have won a piece because of the pin. But White wins a piece just the same by now playing 13 P—KN4! for if 13 . . . PxP; 14 NxP/N4. This explains Black's collapse.

13 P—KN4!	P—B4
14 PxN	Resigns

42

RUY LOPEZ

Black's mistakes: Black starts out with a cramped development (3 . . . P—Q3). To this he adds two serious losses of time—8 . . . B—N4?? and 9 . . . P—Q4??

White's refutation: Thanks to Black's neglected development, White makes good use of his superior development to win a piece by a clever mate threat.

	WHITE	BLACK
1	P—K4	P—K4
2	N—KB3	N—QB3
3	B—N5	P—Q3
4	P—Q4	PxP
5	NxP	B—Q2
6	BxN	PxB
7	N—QB3	B—K2
8	Q—B3!	B—N4??
9	P—K5!	P—Q4??
10	P—K6!	Resigns

(Position after 10 P—K6!)

The point of White's splendid 10 P—K6! is that it wins a piece by the mate threat. For example, 10 . . . PxP; 11 Q—R5ch—or 10 . . . BxP; 11 NxB, PxN; 12 Q—R5ch etc.

GIUOCO PIANO

White's mistakes: White neglects his development by moving his King Knight twice, his Queen Knight twice, his King Bishop twice, and throwing in some useless or harmful Pawn moves. In all this bustle, he forgets to castle his King into safety.

Black's refutation: Realizing that his pieces have much more scope, Black is alert to the opportunity of making good use of the half-open King Bishop file.

	WHITE	BLACK
1	P—K4	P—K4
2	N—KB3	N—QB3
3	B—B4	B—B4
4	P—B3	B—N3
5	P—Q4	Q—K2
6	P—Q5	N—Q1
7	B—K2?	P—Q3
8	P—KR3?	P—KB4
9	B—KN5	N—KB3
10	QN—Q2	Castles
11	N—R4?	PxP
12	NxP?	. . .

(Position after 12 NxP?)

Usually it is good policy to rely on a pin. Not so here, where Black has thought up a devilish way to break the pin.

12	...	NxN!!
13	BxQ	BxPch
14	K—B1	N—N6 mate

KING'S GAMBIT DECLINED
(in effect)

Black's mistakes: Instead of castling into a fierce attack at move 6, Black should have disposed of White's dangerous King Bishop with 6 . . . N—QR4. The greedy expedition 7 . . . N—KN5? and 8 . . . NxRP? only makes matters worse.

White's refutation: White builds up an ideal attacking position against the Black King.

WHITE	BLACK
1 P—K4	P—K4
2 B—B4	N—KB3
3 N—QB3	B—B4
4 P—Q3	P—Q3
5 P—B4	N—B3
6 P—B5	Castles?
7 N—B3	N—KN5?
8 R—B1	NxP?

(Position after 8 . . . NxP?)

Black innocently awaits 9 NxN?, Q—R5ch etc. Instead, White disregards the obnoxious Knight and goes right after Black's King.

9 N—KN5!	NxR
10 Q—R5	P—KR3
11 NxP	RxN
12 QxRch	K—R2
13 B—KN5!!	Resigns

46

If 13 . . . PxB; 14 Q—R5 mate. If 13 . . . QxB; 14 Q—N8 mate. If 13 . . . Q—R1; 14 Q—N6 mate.

RUY LOPEZ

White's mistakes: White takes time to win and hold a Pawn (5 PxP and 11 N—R4), and then loses more time (8 N—QR4? and 9 NxB) to get rid of Black's dangerous King Bishop.

Black's refutation: Making good use of his superior development and open lines, Black pushes his attack to a victorious finish.

	WHITE	BLACK
1	P—K4	P—K4
2	N—KB3	N—QB3
3	B—N5	P—B4
4	N—B3	N—B3
5	PxP	B—B4
6	Castles	Castles
7	R—K1	P—Q3
8	N—QR4?	P—K5!
9	NxB	PxQN
10	BxN	PxB
11	N—R4	P—N4!!
12	PxP e.p.	N—N5!
13	PxPch	K—N2!
14	P—KN3	Q—Q5
15	Q—K2	RxP
16	QxP	R—B8 dbl ch!!

(Position after 16 . . . R—B8 dbl ch!!)

Black's sweeping double check forces White to resign, for if 17 KxR, Q—B7 mate, or 17 K—N2, Q—B7ch (or 17 . . . Q—N8ch); 18 K—R3, QxRP mate. Note how effectively Black's masterly 11 . . . P—N4!! leads to the devastating attack on the King Bishop file.

KING'S INDIAN DEFENSE

Black's mistake: By making three moves with his King Knight, Black loses invaluable time in the opening.

White's refutation: White quickly utilizes his gain in time to set up a devastating attack.

WHITE	BLACK
1 P—Q4	N—KB3
2 N—KB3	P—KN3
3 B—N5	N—K5
4 B—B4	B—N2

5 QN—Q2	NxN
6 QxN	P—Q3
7 B—KR6!	Castles
8 P—KR4!	N—Q2
9 P—R5	N—B3
10 PxP	B—B4

Despair. He sees that after 10 . . . BPxP; 11 BxB, KxB; 12 Q—R6ch followed by P—KN4 White's attack must succeed in the long run.

11 PxRPch	K—R1
12 BxBch	KxB
13 Q—N5ch	B—N3
14 N—R4	Q—K1

(Position after 14 . . . Q—K1)

The maneuver that was adopted here by White (P—KR4–5 to open the King Rook file) is one you can often use successfully when you're ahead in development. Once you have opened the file, the resulting attack is often quickly decisive.

15 P—R8/Qch!   Resigns

For if 15 . . . RxQ; 16 N—B5ch, K—N1; 17 RxRch,
KxR; 18 Q—R6ch and 19 Q—N7 mate.

IRREGULAR DEFENSE

Black's mistakes: Black's development is much too passive
—2 . . . N—Q2 instead of 2 . . . N—KB3, and 3 . . . P—
KN3? instead of 3 . . . P—K4.

White's refutation: Finding Black's Queen hemmed in and
unable to protect its King Knight 4 square, White plays
4 N—N5 to start a slashing combination that wins Black's
Queen.

WHITE	BLACK
1 P—K4	P—Q3
2 B—B4	N—Q2
3 N—KB3	P—KN3?
4 N—N5	N—R3??

A terrible blunder that loses the Queen in a novel manner.
However, 4 . . . P—K3 doesn't look inviting: 5 BxP!, PxB;
6 NxKP, Q—K2; 7 NxPch followed by 8 NxR.

5 BxPch	NxB
6 N—K6	Resigns

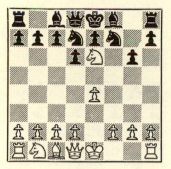

(Position after 6 N—K6)

As a result of this clever combination, White wins the Black Queen. The method White selected drastically highlights his superiority in development.

FRENCH DEFENSE

Black's mistake: It cannot be emphasized too often that playing the Knight to King Bishop 3 is the best protection for the castled King-side position. Black violates this common-sense rule by playing 5 . . . N—K2?

White's refutation: White immediately pins the Knight with 6 B—KN5 and continues to assemble overwhelming force on the King-side.

WHITE	BLACK
1 P—K4	P—K3
2 P—Q4	P—Q4
3 N—QB3	PxP

4 NxP	B—Q3
5 B—Q3	N—K2?
6 B—KN5	Castles?

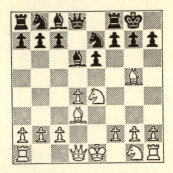

(Position after 6 . . . Castles?)

White's pieces are perfectly poised for an over-whelming onslaught on Black's defenseless King.

7 N—B6ch!	PxN

Or 7 . . . K—R1; 8 Q—R5, P—KR3; 9 BxP, PxN; 10 B—N7 dbl ch!, KxB; 11 Q—R7 mate.

8 BxBP	Q—Q2
9 BxPch!	KxB
10 Q—R5ch	K—N1
11 Q—R8 mate	

SICILIAN DEFENSE

Black's mistakes: Black plays a constricting defense, and fails to hit out for freedom by 7 . . . P—QN4! Later on he has no good freeing move.

White's refutation: White's rapid and aggressive development puts him in a position to exploit Black's 14 . . . N/Q2—B3??

	WHITE	BLACK
1	P—K4	P—QB4
2	N—KB3	P—Q3
3	P—Q4	PxP
4	NxP	N—KB3
5	P—KB3	P—K4
6	N—N5	P—QR3
7	N/N5—B3	QN—Q2?
8	P—QR4!	B—K2
9	N—R3!	Castles
10	N—B4!	N—K1
11	N—Q5!	P—B4
12	PxP	RxP
13	B—Q3	R—B1
14	B—K3	N/Q2—B3??

Black's last move looks perfectly natural. Yet Black's Knight had an important job at Queen 2: preventing White from playing B—QN6. And so White is now able to score a decisive material gain.

(Position after 14 . . . N/Q2—B3)

15	B—QN6!	Q—Q2
16	B—KB5!	Resigns

For if 16 . . . QxB; 17 NxBch wins the Queen.

DUTCH DEFENSE

Black's mistake: By playing 6 . . . PxP?? (instead of 6 . . . P—K6!) Black allows the opening of the King Bishop file.

White's refutation: White builds up pressure on the open King Bishop file and develops rapidly in order to menace the Black King.

	WHITE	BLACK
1	P—Q4	P—KB4
2	P—K4	PxP
3	N—QB3	N—KB3
4	P—KN4!?	P—Q4
5	P—N5	N—N1

6	P—B3!	PxP??
7	QxP	P—K3
8	B—Q3	P—KN3
9	KN—K2	Q—K2
10	B—KB4!	P—B3
11	B—K5!	B—N2
12	Q—N3!	N—QR3
13	Castles KR	B—Q2
14	B—Q6	Q—Q1
15	Q—B4!	Resigns

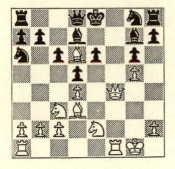

(Position after 15 Q—B4!)

White has intensified his grip on the King Bishop file until he now threatens 16 Q—B7 mate or 16 Q—B8ch, BxQ; 17 RxB mate. So powerful is White's position that Black has no satisfactory defense.

RUY LOPEZ

Black's mistakes: Black wastes time with 3 . . . N—Q5, and, even more critically, with 8 . . . N—B3?

White's refutation: White's forceful Queen moves soon reduce Black to helplessness.

WHITE	BLACK
1 P—K4	P—K4
2 N—KB3	N—QB3
3 B—N5	N—Q5
4 NxN	PxN
5 P—Q3	P—QR3
6 B—QB4	P—QN4
7 B—N3	B—N2
8 Castles	N—B3?
9 P—K5	N—N1
10 Q—N4!	P—N3
11 B—N5!	B—K2
12 Q—B4!	. . .

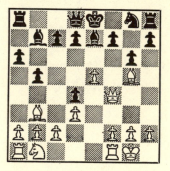

(Position after 12 Q—B4!)

White's mating threat cannot be met satisfactorily, for if 12 . . . P—Q4; 13 PxP e.p. is decisive.

12 ...	P—KB3
13 PxP	BxBP

If 13 . . . NxP; 14 R—K1 wins the Black Knight.

14 BxN	Resigns

He has no good move (if 14 . . . BxB??; 15 Q—B7 mate).

ALEKHINE'S DEFENSE

White's mistakes: White's 4 B—K2? (instead of 4 P—Q4!) is extraordinarily careless. 5 B—B1? proves to be a fatal loss of time, exposing White's King to a decisive attack.

Black's refutation: Black takes alert advantage of his opponent's shortcomings, beginning with his sharp and powerful 4 . . . N—B5!

WHITE	BLACK
1 P—K4	N—KB3
2 P—K5	N—Q4
3 N—KB3	P—Q3
4 B—K2?	N—B5!
5 B—B1?	. . .

He had nothing better than 5 Castles, though after 5 . . .
PxP; 6 NxP, Q—Q4 (threatens mate) ; 7 N—KB3, B—N5
Black has a mighty initiative.

5	. . .	PxP
6	NxP	Q—Q4!
7	N—KB3	Q—K5ch!
8	B—K2	NxPch
9	K—B1	B—R6
10	P—Q3	. . .

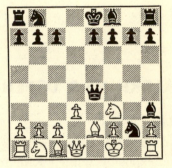

(Position after 10 P—Q3)

Black's fierce onrush has decided the game in his
favor. So powerful is the position of his pieces
that he has a forced mate in two moves, based on
a crushing discovered check.

10	. . .	N—R5 dis ch
11	K—K1	NxN mate

Another way was 11 K—N1, Q—KN5 mate.

QUEEN'S PAWN OPENING

White's mistakes: White makes altogether too many Pawn moves in the opening (six out of 12 moves). In addition, he misses two surprise moves by Black.

Black's refutation: Black develops quickly and purposefully and doesn't miss a trick. His 9 . . . BxPch! and 12 . . . P—B6!! are alert and decisive.

WHITE	BLACK
1 P—Q4	P—K4?!
2 P—Q5?	P—KB4
3 P—QB4	N—KB3
4 N—QB3	B—B4
5 N—B3	P—Q3
6 P—QR3	Castles
7 P—QN4	B—N3
8 B—N2	P—B5
9 N—KN5?	BxPch!
10 KxB	N—N5ch
11 K—N1	QxN
12 P—KR4	. . .

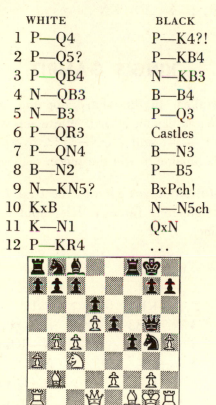

(Position after 12 P—KR4)

Of course, Black can simply retreat his attacked Queen with a winning game. But he has a different move which shatters White's position.

12 ...   P—B6!!

White resigns—a wise decision. If 13 PxQ, P—B7 mate; or 13 BPxP, Q—K6 mate. If 13 NPxP, Q—K6ch; 14 K—N2, Q—B7ch; 15 K—R3, KN moves giving checkmate!

KING'S GAMBIT

White's mistakes: In this sharp opening, mistakes are a luxury that White cannot afford. White sets a trap to win a piece with 6 P—B4? and 7 QN—Q2?, overlooking the fact that he will be unable to win the piece.

Black's refutation: Black ignores the trap and leaps to the attack with frightening ferocity. His rapid development decides the game.

	WHITE	BLACK
1	P—K4	P—K4
2	P—KB4	PxP
3	N—KB3	P—Q4
4	PxP	N—KB3
5	P—Q4	NxP
6	P—B4?	B—QN5ch!
7	QN—Q2?	N—K6!
8	Q—R4ch?	B—Q2

For if 9 QxKB?, N—B7ch wins the Queen for Black.

| 9 Q—N3 | Q—K2 |
| 10 K—B2 | N—Q8ch! |

(Position after 10 . . . N—Q8ch!)

Black plays the attack with real artistry. 11 QxN will not do because of 11 . . . Q—K6 mate. So White chooses a different move, but Black has an even more beautiful refutation in readiness.

| 11 K—N1 | N—B6!! |

So that if 12 PxN, Q—K6 mate.

| 12 P—KR3 | B—R5! |

White resigns; Black has trapped his Queen.

3. How to Win When Your Opponent's Queen Is Out of Play or In Danger

Since the Queen is the most powerful piece on the board, your opponent may ruin his game irretrievably by developing this formidable piece in a faulty way.

Basically there are two types of such situations in which you can expect to profit decisively. In one case (pages 63-73) the hostile Queen has been enticed far from the scene of action. Perhaps your opponent was too greedy; perhaps he has just been careless. At any rate, the absence of the hostile Queen gives you the opportunity for a winning attack. Particularly colorful are those attacks where the hostile Queen has captured two Rooks—with fatal results for your greedy opponent!

The other types of positions to study are those (pages 74-82) where your opponent has developed his Queen prematurely and has exposed her to some winning tactical finesse on your part. Such opportunities for victory arise very often in the opening. Master these simple techniques and you'll win many games more quickly.

CENTER COUNTER GAME

Black's mistakes: Black loses valuable time with his premature Queen moves. Then he increases White's lead in development with the faulty exchange 7 . . . BxN?

White's refutation: White lays a deep plan to entice the Black Queen far from the scene of action, starting with 10 P—R3!

	WHITE	BLACK
1	P—K4	P—Q4
2	PxP	QxP
3	N—QB3	Q—QR4
4	P—Q4	P—QB3
5	N—B3	B—N5
6	B—KB4	P—K3
7	P—KR3	BxN?
8	QxB	B—N5
9	B—K2	N—Q2
10	P—R3!	Castles?

(Position after 10 . . . Castles?)

Black mistakenly thinks that 11 PxB is out of the question. But White, seeing further ahead and relying on his excellent attacking position, has a stunning surprise continuation.

	WHITE	BLACK
11	PxB!!	QxRch
12	K—Q2	QxR
13	QxPch!!	PxQ
14	B—QR6 mate!	

PHILIDOR'S DEFENSE

White's mistakes: White ruins his development by making far too many Queen moves—five out of a total of 13.

Black's refutation: Concentrating on rapid and aggressive development, Black builds up a crushing attack against White's King.

	WHITE	BLACK
1	P—K4	P—K4
2	N—KB3	P—Q3
3	P—Q4	N—KB3
4	PxP	NxP
5	B—QB4	B—K3
6	BxB	PxB
7	Q—K2	P—Q4
8	Q—N5ch?	N—QB3

If now 9 QxNP?, N—N5!; 10 Q—N5ch, P—B3; 11

Q—R4, N—B4!! winning White's Queen, for if 12 QxN, N—Q6ch.

9	N—Q4?	Q—Q2
10	QxNP?	B—N5ch
11	P—QB3	. . .

(Position after 11 P—QB3)

Black has three pieces under attack, yet he has everything under control. He plays the brilliant 11 . . . NxN!! so that if 12 PxB, Castles with the winning threat of . . . N—B7ch or . . . NxP.

11	. . .	NxN!!
12	QxRch	K—B2
13	QxR	Q—N4!!
14	Resigns	

White is helpless against the coming . . . Q—K7 mate.

KING KNIGHT OPENING

White's mistakes: White rightly proceeds energetically against Black's passive defense. However, White makes the mistake of wandering too far afield with his Queen.

Black's refutation: Black conceives a wonderfully ingenious counterattack which at the cost of considerable material leads to a mating position.

	WHITE	BLACK
1	P—K4	P—K4
2	N—KB3	N—QB3
3	B—B4	P—Q3?
4	P—B3	B—N5!
5	Q—N3!?	Q—Q2
6	N—N5	N—R3
7	BxPch?!	NxB
8	NxN	QxN
9	QxP	K—Q2!
10	QxR	Q—QB5!!
11	P—B3	BxP!!
12	PxB	N—Q5!!

Black sees that after 13 PxN, QxBch; 14 K—K2, QxR; 15 P—Q5, QxRPch he will have a winning game. Of course, White can win another piece with 13 P—Q3, but Black is fully prepared with a stunning refutation.

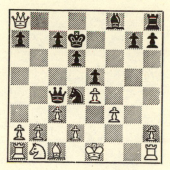

(Position after 12 . . . N—Q5!!)

	WHITE	BLACK
13	P—Q3	QxQP
14	PxN	B—K2!!
15	QxR	B—R5 mate!

GRECO COUNTER GAMBIT

White's mistakes: White tries to win material by a series of greedy Queen moves (7 Q—R5ch etc.).

Black's refutation: In a sequence of extraordinarily brilliant sacrifices, Black squeezes the last drop of advantage out of the position.

	WHITE	BLACK
1	P—K4	P—K4
2	N—KB3	P—KB4
3	PxP	N—QB3
4	B—N5	B—B4
5	BxN	QPxB
6	NxP	BxP
7	Q—R5ch	P—KN3
8	NxNP?!	. . .

(Position after 8 NxNP?!)

Black has worked out a wonderful combination, but all that White sees is that he will be two Pawns up after 8 . . . BxN; 9 QxKB. Instead, Black entices the White Queen far from the scene of action.

8	...	PxN!!
9	QxR	Q—K2ch
10	K—Q1	KBxP!!
11	QxNch	K—Q2!
12	Q—B4	R—K1
13	Resigns	

If 13 P—Q3, Q—K7 mate. If 13 P—Q4, B—N5ch; 14 K—Q2, Q—K6 mate.

VIENNA GAME

Black's mistakes: Black loses valuable time with his wasted Queen moves, so that his King is defenseless.

White's refutation: After developing rapidly by taking advantage of the Black Queen's exile, White organizes a decisive attack.

	WHITE	BLACK
1	P—K4	P—K4
2	N—QB3	N—QB3
3	B—B4	B—B4
4	Q—N4	Q—B3
5	N—Q5!	QxPch
6	K—Q1	K—B1
7	N—R3	Q—Q5
8	P—Q3	B—N3

White threatened 9 P—B3 winning the Queen!

9	R—B1	N—B3
10	RxN!	P—Q3

He sees that 10 . . . PxR is hopeless because of 11 B—R6ch, K—K1; 12 Q—N7 etc.

(Position after 10 . . . P—Q3)

With Black's Queen looking on helplessly, White is ready for the final attack.

11 QxPch!!	KxQ
12 B—KR6ch	K—N1
13 R—N6ch!!	RPxR
14 N—B6 mate	

Or 13 . . . BPxR; 14 N checks giving checkmate!

DANISH GAMBIT

Black's mistakes: Black wastes too much time on Pawn captures and useless Queen moves.

White's refutation: White develops with gain of time to work up a devastating attack.

WHITE	BLACK
1 P—K4	P—K4
2 P—Q4	PxP
3 P—QB3	PxP
4 B—QB4	PxP
5 QBxP	Q—N4?
6 N—KB3!	QxP
7 BxPch!	. . .

For if 7 . . . KxB; 8 R—N1, Q—R6; 9 N—N5ch.

7 . . .	K—Q1
8 R—N1	B—N5ch
9 N—B3	Q—R6

10	R—N3	Q—R3
11	Q—N3	BxNch
12	QxB	N—KB3

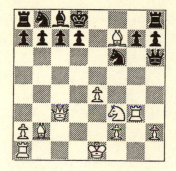

(Position after 12 . . . N—KB3)

White's magnificently developed pieces are poised for the kill. Watch how White knocks Black's only two developed pieces out of action.

13	R—N6!!	PxR
14	QxNch!!	PxQ
15	BxP mate	

FRENCH DEFENSE

Black's mistakes: Black wastes time with too many Queen moves and plays the inexact 6 . . . KN—K2? (instead of 6 . . . PxP!).

White's refutation: White develops his pieces cleverly to harry the Black Queen with gain of time.

	WHITE	BLACK
1	P—K4	P—K3
2	P—Q4	P—Q4
3	P—K5	P—QB4
4	P—QB3	N—QB3
5	N—B3	Q—N3
6	B—Q3	KN—K2?
7	PxP!	Q—B2
8	N—R3!	NxP
9	N—QN5!	NxBch
10	QxN	QxP
11	B—K3	. . .

(Position after 11 B—K3)

Now White's superior development pays off. If
11 . . . Q—B3; 12 N—K5! wins Black's Queen.
Black saves his Queen, but White drives her far
afield and works up a mating attack.

11	. . .	P—Q5
12	BxP	Q—B3
13	N—K5!	QxNP
14	N—Q6ch	K—Q1

15 B—N6ch!   Resigns

If 15 . . . PxB; 16 N/Q6xBP dbl ch and mate next move.

GRUENFELD DEFENSE

White's mistakes: Four of White's first eight moves are Queen moves. His Queen ends up at Queen Knight 7, badly out of play.

Black's refutation: Black develops his pieces with gain of time against White's Queen. He then proceeds to work up a devastating attack.

WHITE	BLACK
1 P—Q4	N—KB3
2 P—QB4	P—KN3
3 N—QB3	P—Q4
4 Q—N3	PxP
5 QxBP	B—K3
6 Q—N5ch?	N—B3
7 N—B3	N—Q4
8 QxP??	N/Q4—N5!

(Position after 8 . . . N/Q4—N5!)

Black threatens to win White's Queen with . . .
QR—N1. This explains why White now plays 9
B—B4 and why Black replies 9 . . . B—R3!! with
a view to 10 BxB, QR—N1. But this sly idea is
only the beginning of Black's brilliant plan.

9	B—B4	B—R3!!
10	BxP	NxQP!!
11	BxQ	N/Q5—B7ch
12	K—Q1	RxBch
13	N—Q5	BxN
14	Q—B7	BxN dis ch
15	QxRch	KxQ
16	KPxB	K—B2

White resigns, for if 17 QR—N1, R—Q1ch; 18 K—K2,
R—Q7 mate.

CARO-KANN DEFENSE

White's mistakes: White indulges in a useless Queen check
(8 Q—N5ch?) in order to capture a tainted Pawn (9 Qx
BP??).

Black's refutation: Black deliberately sets a trap for White's
Queen, and the trap works!

	WHITE	BLACK
1	P—K4	P—QB3
2	P—Q4	P—Q4
3	P—K5	B—B4

4 B—Q3	BxB
5 QxB	P—K3
6 N—K2	P—QB4
7 P—QB3	N—K2!
8 Q—N5ch?	Q—Q2

Leaving White nothing better than 9 QxQch. Instead, White rushes to his doom.

9 QxBP??	N—B4!

(Position after 9 . . . N—B4!)

White resigns, for after 10 Q—R5 (forced), Black plays 10 . . . P—QN3! and White's Queen is trapped!

BENONI COUNTER GAMBIT

Black's mistakes: Black's premature Queen moves (instead of 2 . . . P—K3 and 3 . . . BxP) create a suspicion that the Queen may be endangered later on. With the doubtful 4 . . .

P—K4? (allowing White to sink his Queen Knight at Queen 5) the suspicion becomes a certainty.

White's refutation: White sees in a flash that the powerful posting of his Queen Knight at Queen 5 can be the prelude to a forced win of Black's Queen.

WHITE	BLACK
1 P—Q4	P—QB4
2 PxP	Q—R4ch?
3 N—QB3	QxBP
4 P—K4	P—K4?
5 N—B3	P—Q3
6. N—Q5!	N—K2?

(Position after 6 . . . N—K2?)

Black has overlooked the subtle threat with which White is operating. As the position stands, White wins the Queen by force.

7 P—QN4!   Q—B3

The only square left for the Black Queen.

> 8 B—QN5!   Resigns

For if 8 . . . QxB; 9 N—B7ch wins the Queen.

CENTER GAME

White's mistakes: White loses valuable time for development by bringing out his Queen much too early. He makes
a second mistake in moving a Pawn (7 P—QB3) instead of
developing a piece (7 B—Q2 or 7 N—QB3). And he makes
a final, immediately disastrous mistake in placing his Queen
where it is exposed to a murderous double attack.

Black's refutation: Black gains time for rapid development
by nimbly attacking White's Queen with his minor pieces.
But Black knows what to do with his gain of time—he utilizes
it for a stunning tactical finish.

WHITE	BLACK
1 P—K4	P—K4
2 P—Q4?	PxP
3 QxP	N—QB3!
4 Q—K3	N—B3
5 B—B4	N—K4
6 B—N3	B—N5ch
7 P—QB3?	B—B4

If 8 QxB??, N—Q6ch. White avoids this, but falls into
something just as bad.

8 Q—N3??	BxPch!!
9 Resigns	

(Position after 8 . . . BxPch!!)

Black wins the Queen by force, for if 9 KxB, NxPch—or if 9 QxB, N—Q6ch. Thus Black has brought to a logical and convincing conclusion his indicated procedure for hounding the White Queen.

KING'S GAMBIT

White's mistakes: White not only plays out his Queen prematurely, but buries his King Bishop with 4 N—K2? and ruins his game irretrievably with 6 P—KN3??

Black's refutation: Black neatly combines development with hounding of White's Queen.

WHITE	BLACK
1 P—K4	P—K4
2 P—KB4	PxP
3 Q—B3?	N—QB3
4 N—K2?	B—B4
5 P—Q3	P—KN4!
6 P—KN3??	N—K4!

This leaves White without a good reply, for example 7 Q—R5, N—KB3!; 8 Q—R6 (or 8 QxNP?, N—B6ch), N—B6ch; 9 K—Q1, N—N5; 10 Q—N7, N—B7 mate.

7 Q—N2   P—B6

(Position after 7 . . . P—B6)

Black's last move forces the win of a piece, so White resigns. Black has taken full advantage of White's slovenly opening play.

QUEEN'S GAMBIT DECLINED

Black's mistakes: Black makes several early Queen moves to win a Pawn. This leaves him in an uncomfortable position, in which he fails to take proper defensive measures.

White's refutation: White gives up a Pawn for rapid development of his pieces. Note how he immediately pounces on Black's 11 . . . K—B2??

	WHITE	BLACK
1	P—Q4	P—Q4
2	P—QB4	P—QB3
3	N—QB3	P—K3
4	P—K4	PxKP
5	NxP	B—N5ch
6	B—Q2!?	QxP
7	BxB	QxNch
8	B—K2	N—QR3
9	B—Q6!	N—K2
10	N—B3	P—B3
11	Castles	K—B2??

Black is blissfully unaware of the danger to his Queen.
He should play 11 . . . P—K4! making . . . Q—B5 possible.

| 12 | B—Q3! | Resigns |

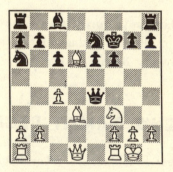

(Position after 12 B—Q3!)

Why does Black resign? Because his Queen has
only one move: 12 . . . Q—N5. But then comes
13 N—K5ch! winning the Queen. White lost no
time taking advantage of Black's blunder.

SICILIAN DEFENSE

White's mistake: White uses his Queen to defend a mere Pawn (12 Q—N3?). When the plan fails miserably, he sends his Queen far afield.

Black's refutation: Black gains considerable time by harrying White's Queen and finally wins decisive material.

	WHITE	BLACK
1	P—K4	P—QB4
2	P—QN4	PxP
3	N—KB3	P—Q4!
4	PxP	N—KB3!
5	P—QR3	NxP
6	PxP	NxP
7	P—Q4	B—B4
8	N—R3	P—K3
9	B—QN5ch	QN—B3
10	P—B3	P—QR3!
11	B—K2	N—Q4
12	Q—N3?	NxBP!

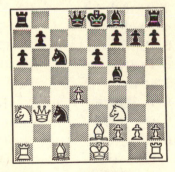

(Position after 12 . . . NxBP!)

Black's last move has caught White off base, for if 13 QxN, B—QN5 wins the Queen. Rather than remain two Pawns down, White tries to get a Pawn back—but watch what happens to his Queen!

| 13 QxNP?? | N—R4 |
| 14 Q—N2 | QR—N1 |

White resigns, for if 15 Q—Q2, N—N6 wins easily.

RETI OPENING

White's mistakes: White's 9 Q—R4? is pointless, as the Queen is bound to be driven away sooner or later with loss of time. With 12 B—QR3?? White courts disaster.

Black's refutation: Black demonstrates efficiently that 9 Q—R4? is risky as well as pointless.

WHITE	BLACK
1 N—KB3	P—Q4
2 P—KN3	N—KB3
3 B—N2	P—KN3
4 Castles	B—N2
5 P—B4	P—Q5
6 P—K3	P—B4
7 PxP	PxP
8 P—Q3	N—B3
9 Q—R4?	Castles
10 P—QN4	N—Q2!
11 QN—Q2	P—QR4!
12 B—QR3??	. . .

White relies on the fact that 12 . . . PxP is "impossible."
Beware of "impossible" moves!

| 12 . . . | PxP!! |
| 13 QxR | N—N3 |

(Position after 13 . . . N—N3)

And now White finds, to his chagrin and amaze-
ment, that his Queen is trapped! Black's tenth to
thirteenth moves form a study in purposeful, forceful play. White resigns.

4. How to Win by Taking Your Opponent by Surprise

A surprise move is one of the most potent ways to beat your opponent quickly. Sometimes this comes about in the form of a threat which he overlooks (pages 85-89). In that case he unknowingly gives you the opportunity to carry out a decisive threat.

More subtle are those surprise moves (pages 91-104) in which you interpolate a stunning reply against some preconceived notion of your opponent's. He is going along pleasantly, carrying out his plan, when suddenly bang!—your move not only ruins his plan, but also wins the game for you. The games on pages 91-98, in which the winner calmly leaves his Queen to be captured, are particularly entertaining.

Finally, there is an important class of surprise moves (pages 105-114) which have to be improvised on the spur of the moment. This happens in positions in which your opponent is apparently safe; then, with one false step he leaves himself wide open to a subtle winning move. If you're alertly poised for your chance, you can win the game on the spot or else force your opponent's resignation in jig time.

CATALAN OPENING

White's mistakes: White's 6 PxP? only develops the Black Bishop with gain of time for Black. And 7 B—N2? (instead of 7 Q—R4ch and 8 QxBP) sadly misses the threat.

Black's refutation: Black is very alert in sensing the possibilities resulting from 7 B—N2?

WHITE	BLACK
1 P—Q4	N—KB3
2 P—QB4	P—K3
3 N—KB3	P—Q4
4 P—KN3	PxP
5 QN—Q2	P—B4
6 PxP?	BxP
7 B—N2?	. . .

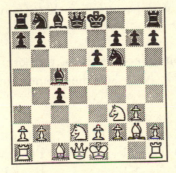

(Position after 7 B—N2?)

On the surface this looks like a perfectly satisfactory developing move. That is why Black deserves great credit for finding the subtle flaw in this move.

85

7 ...		BxPch!!
8	KxB	N—N5ch

Now everything is clear: if 9 K—B1, N—K6ch winning the Queen—and if 9 K—N1, Q—N3ch forcing mate.

9	K—K1	N—K6

White resigns, for after 10 Q—R4ch, B—Q2 his Queen is trapped! (If 11 Q—N4 or Q—R3, N—B7ch.)

DUTCH DEFENSE

White's mistakes: White commits himself too soon in the center with 7 P—B5? and 9 P—B4? Then, when the situation has deteriorated because of these moves, he blunders with 10 N—Q2?

Black's refutation: Black develops purposefully with a view to King-side attack. Note how he pounces on White's faulty tenth move.

WHITE		BLACK
1 P—Q4		P—K3
2 N—KB3		P—KB4
3 P—KN3		N—KB3
4 B—N2		B—K2
5 Castles		Castles
6 P—B4		P—Q4
7 P—B5?		N—K5

8	N—K5	N—Q2
9	P—B4?	Q—K1!
10	N—Q2?	

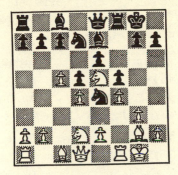

(Position after 10 N—Q2?)

If White had fully appreciated the sinister implications of 9 . . . Q—K1! he would have played 10 P—K3. As the position stands, Black can carry out a splendid combination.

10	. . .	N/Q2xP!
11	PxN	BxPch
12	K—R1	NxPch!
13	Resigns	

If 13 PxN, Q—R4ch leads to mate.

RUY LOPEZ

Black's mistakes: Black plays a cramped defense which gives his pieces very little scope. He must therefore play with great care later on—say 12 . . . N—Q2 followed by 13 . . . B—B3.

Instead he completely misses the point, overlooking White's threat at move 15.

White's refutation: White develops his pieces forcefully and takes advantage of Black's carelessness to establish a powerful bind on the hostile position.

	WHITE	BLACK
1	P—K4	P—K4
2	N—KB3	N—QB3
3	B—N5	N—B3
4	N—B3	P—Q3?
5	P—Q4!	B—Q2
6	Castles	B—K2
7	R—K1	PxP
8	NxP	NxN
9	QxN	BxB
10	NxB	Castles
11	Q—B3	P—QR3
12	N—Q4	R—K1?
13	N—B5	B—B1
14	B—N5	RxP??

(Position after 14 . . . RxP??)

88

Black reckons only on 15 BxN, RxRch!—or 15 RxR, NxR; 16 BxQ, NxQ. However, White has steered for this position, relying on the threat of 15 N—R6ch!, which cannot be answered by 15 . . . K—R1 because of 16 NxPch.

| 15 N—R6ch! | PxN |
| 16 BxN | Resigns |

White threatens 17 Q—KN3ch and also attacks Black's Queen and Rook.

DUTCH DEFENSE

Black's mistakes: By playing 3 . . . P—Q4! Black could have safely barricaded the position. But the decisive error is 10 . . . Q—K2?? Instead, 10 . . . BxN! beats off the attack (11 PxB, R—B4! or 11 QxB, N—B3).

White's refutation: White concentrates his attacking forces to make a Queen sacrifice possible.

WHITE	BLACK
1 P—Q4	P—KB4
2 N—KB3	P—K3
3 N—B3	N—KB3
4 B—N5	B—K2
5 BxN	BxB
6 P—K4	PxP
7 NxP	P—QN3
8 B—Q3	B—N2

9 N—K5	Castles
10 Q—R5	Q—K2??

(Position after 10 . . . Q—K2??)

White's last move carried a threat so subtle that Black has completely overlooked it. White has a forced mate, beginning with a fantastic Queen sacrifice.

11 QxPch!!!	KxQ
12 NxB dbl ch	K—R3

If 12 . . . K—R1; 13 N—N6 mate.

13 N/K5—N4ch	K—N4
14 P—B4ch	Resigns

If 13 . . . K—R5; 14 P—KN3ch, K—R6; 15 B—B1ch, B—N7; 16 N—B2 mate.

And after 13 . . . KxP White mates by 14 P—KN3ch, K—B6 (or 14 . . . K—N4; 15 P—KR4 mate); 15 Castles KR mate!

BUDAPEST DEFENSE

White's mistakes: White wastes time with 3 P—Q5 instead of the simple and excellent alternative 3 PxP. But his real mistake is 4 B—N5??; White is completely oblivious of Black's smashing reply.

Black's refutation: Black takes advantage of White's feeble third move to develop his King Bishop effectively. Then he operates most imaginatively to foresee an astounding checkmate.

	WHITE	BLACK
1	P—Q4	N—KB3
2	P—QB4	P—K4
3	P—Q5	B—B4!
4	B—N5??	N—K5!!

Already decisive. White's feeble "best" is 5 B—K3, when Black gets a winning game with 5 . . . BxB; 6 PxB, Q—R5ch; 7 P—KN3, NxP etc.

(Position after 4 . . . N—K5!!)

Black's ingenious Knight move comes as a complete surprise to White.

5 BxQ   BxP mate

SICILIAN DEFENSE

Black's mistakes: Instead of the aggressive 3 . . . P—Q4! Black plays the passive 3 . . . P—Q3. With his fifth and sixth moves he places altogether too much reliance on the power of the pin.

White's refutation: White realizes that Black is entering on complications too soon. Keeping his eye on the hostile King, White sees that he can win by a pseudo-sacrifice of his Queen.

WHITE	BLACK
1 P—K4	P—QB4
2 N—KB3	N—QB3
3 P—B3	P—Q3?
4 P—Q4	PxP
5 PxP	B—N5?
6 P—Q5	N—K4??

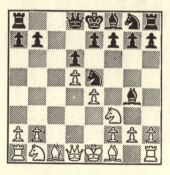

(Position after 6 . . . N—K4??)

White rocks Black back on his heels by playing a completely unexpected reply. White's combination is based on the fact that Black's King is vulnerable.

7 NxN!!   . . .

If now 7 . . . BxQ; 8 B—QN5ch, Q—Q2; 9 BxQch, K—Q1; 10 NxPch, KxB; 11 KxB! with an overwhelming plus in material for White.

7 . . .	Q—R4ch
8 B—Q2	BxQ
9 BxQ	PxN
10 B—N5 mate!	

CENTER GAME

Black's mistakes: Black makes too many Pawn moves and neglects to bring out his King-side pieces, deferring castling indefinitely. Worst of all, he quite fails to fathom White's devilish trap on move 8 (instead of playing 8 . . . P—Q4).

White's refutation: White gets a big lead in development and then sets a remarkably fine trap with 8 P—K5!! It takes imagination of a high order to foresee the consequences of this move.

WHITE	BLACK
1 P—K4	P—K4
2 P—Q4	PxP
3 B—QB4	P—QB4?
4 N—KB3	P—Q3

5	Castles	N—QB3
6	P—B3	P—Q6 '
7	R—K1	B—N5?
8	P—K5!!	NxP??

(Position after 8 . . . NxP??)

White now plays the brilliant 9 NxN!!, so as to play 10 QxB (winning a piece) in answer to 9 . . . PxN. Instead, Black prefers to win the Queen, which has even more drastic consequences.

9	NxN!!	BxQ
10	B—QN5ch	K—K2
11	B—N5ch	P—B3

If 11 . . . N—B3; 12 N—N6 mate!

12	N—N6 dbl ch	K—B2
13	NxR mate!	

CENTER COUNTER GAME

Black's mistakes: Black loses valuable time with his early Queen moves and then fails to realize that his development is not good enough to support the pin.

White's refutation: As so often happens, White's startling resource arises from a surprise checking possibility.

WHITE	BLACK
1 P—K4	P—Q4
2 PxP	QxP
3 N—QB3	Q—Q1
4 P—Q4	N—QB3
5 N—B3	B—N5
6 P—Q5!	N—K4??

Provoked by White's last move, Black thinks he can play the Knight to King 4 with impunity.

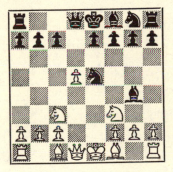

(Position after 6 . . . N—K4??)

Obviously, thinks Black, White must not play 7 NxN for this would lose the Queen. Yet here is the rare exception, on which White immediately pounces.

| 7 NxN!! | BxQ |
| 8 B—QN5ch | Resigns |

Black must play 8 . . . P—QB3 and after 9 PxP he is curiously helpless against the possibility of 10 PxP dis ch or 10 P—B7 dis ch. For example: 9 . . . B—N5; 10 PxP dis ch, B—Q2; 11 BxBch, QxB; 12 PxR/Qch, Q—Q1; 13 Q—B6ch and mate next move.

VIENNA GAME

Black's mistakes: Black gets a bad game with 3 . . . P—Q3? (instead of the vigorous 3 . . . P—Q4!) and 7 . . . N—KR4?? moving the Knight needlessly and exposing the Black King to a vicious attack.

White's refutation: White, relying on his superior development, sees a chance for a remarkable sacrifice.

WHITE	BLACK
1 P—K4	P—K4
2 N—QB3	N—KB3
3 P—B4	P—Q3?
4 N—B3	N—B3
5 B—B4	B—N5
6 Castles	B—K2
7 P—Q3	N—KR4??
8 PxP	NxP

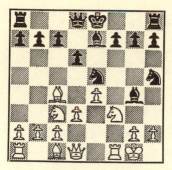

(Position after 8 . . . NxP)

Black is much too cocky in thinking that he can rely on the pin. It is superior development that enables White to concoct a magnificent Queen sacrifice that forces checkmate.

9	NxN!!	BxQ
10	BxPch	K—B1
11	BxN dis ch	B—B3
12	RxBch!!	PxR

If 12 . . . QxR; 13 N—Q7ch wins.

13	B—R6ch	K—K2
14	N—Q5ch	K—K3
15	B—B7ch!	KxN
16	P—B3	Resigns

White mates next move.

SICILIAN DEFENSE

Black's mistake: Black does well enough against White's time-wasting B—Q3—B2 maneuver. But he goes grievously astray with the slovenly 10 . . . PxP?? (instead of the alert 10 . . . NxNch!).

White's refutation: White's trappy 9 B—R4ch! sets the stage for Black's subsequent blunder. At move 11, White applies an ancient, effective theme.

	WHITE	BLACK
1	P—K4	P—QB4
2	N—KB3	P—Q3
3	P—B3	N—KB3!
4	B—Q3!?	N—B3
5	B—B2	B—N5
6	P—KR3	B—R4
7	P—Q4	P—K3
8	P—Q5	N—K4
9	B—R4ch!	N/B3—Q2
10	PxP	PxP??

(Position after 10 . . . PxP??)

In the play that follows, White adopts a familiar idea with an amusing facet.

11 NxN!!	BxQ
12 BxNch	QxB

The point is that if 12 . . . K—K2; 13 B—KN5 mate.

13 NxQ	B—B7
14 NxB	Resigns

Black remains a piece down.

NIMZOINDIAN DEFENSE

Black's mistakes: Black's 5 . . . Q—R4? starts a faulty plan which is completed with 7 . . . NxP??

White's refutation: White cleverly refutes Black's inadequate plan with two surprises at moves 7 and 8.

WHITE	BLACK
1 P—Q4	N—KB3
2 P—QB4	P—K3
3 N—QB3	B—N5
4 Q—N3	P—B4
5 P—QR3!	Q—R4?
6 B—Q2!	. . .

Naturally, White avoids 6 PxB?, QxR etc.

```
6 . . .                    N—QB3
7 Q—Q1                     NxP??
```

Not liking 7 . . . BxN; 8 BxB, Q—Q1; 9 P—Q5, which completely disorganizes his game, Black sets a trap.

(Position after 7 . . . NxP??)

White is too cagey to succumb to 8 PxB?, QxR!; 9 QxQ, N—B7ch; 10 K—Q1, NxQ leaving Black the Exchange ahead. Instead, White wins a piece.

```
8 P—K3!                    Resigns
```

White wins a piece, for example 8 . . . N—B3; 9 PxB (now feasible!) or 8 . . . BxN; 9 BxB winning the Knight because Black's Queen is attacked.

CARO-KANN DEFENSE

Black's mistakes: Black goes wrong in entering on premature complications and relying on early Queen moves. But his fatal mistake is to think he can grab a piece and get away with it (instead of healthy development with 8 . . . B—K2).

White's refutation: White relies on an amazing Queen sacrifice, followed by a devastating double check.

	WHITE	BLACK
1	P—K4	P—QB3
2	P—Q4	P—Q4
3	N—QB3	PxP
4	NxP	N—B3
5	Q—Q3!?	P—K4?
6	PxP	Q—R4ch?
7	B—Q2	QxKP
8	Castles!!	NxN?

If 8 . . . QxN; 9 R—K1 wins the Queen.

(Position after 8 . . . NxN?)

Unbelievable as it may sound, White has a forced mate. It is based on a particularly sly double check.

9 Q—Q8ch!! KxQ
10 B—N5 dbl ch Resigns

A great light dawns. If 10 . . . K—K1; 11 R—Q8 mate. If 10 . . . K—B2; 11 B—Q8 mate.

TWO KNIGHTS' DEFENSE

Black's mistake: Black is too greedy and thinks he can remain a piece ahead at move 9.

White's refutation: White neatly lays the groundwork (7 Q—R5ch, P—N3) for an unexpected check at move 10 which wins the game for him.

WHITE	BLACK
1 P—K4	P—K4
2 N—KB3	N—QB3
3 B—B4	N—B3
4 P—Q4	PxP
5 NxP	NxP
6 BxPch	KxB
7 Q—R5ch	P—N3
8 Q—Q5ch	K—N2
9 NxN	N—B3?

Simply 9 . . . NPxN gives Black a playable game.

(Position after 9 . . . N—B3?)

Black expects to gain time with this attack on the White Queen so that he can remain a piece ahead. Or if 10 NxQ, NxQ with the same result. But White has seen further ahead and has a resource which his opponent has completely overlooked.

10	B—R6ch!	KxB
11	Q—Q2ch	Resigns

White has saved his own Queen and can now continue with 12 NxQ.

QUEEN'S GAMBIT DECLINED

Black's mistake: Intent on counterplay, Black completely overlooks a dazzling attacking resource when he plays 10 . . . Q—R4ch?? instead of 10 . . . B—K2.

White's refutation: With Black's Queen voluntarily drawn off from the defense, White sees an opportunity for an amazing Queen sacrifice.

	WHITE	BLACK
1	P—Q4	P—Q4
2	P—QB4	P—K3
3	N—QB3	N—KB3
4	N—B3	B—K2
5	B—N5	QN—Q2
6	P—K3	Castles
7	Q—B2	P—B4
8	BPxP	NxP
9	NxN	BxB
10	P—KR4!	Q—R4ch??
11	P—QN4!!	PxNP

(Position after 11 . . . PxNP)

Black is prepared for 12 NxB, which threatens mate and seemingly wins a piece. On 12 NxB Black intends 12 . . . P—N6ch forcing the White Queen to Queen 2 or Queen Bishop 3 and thus making it possible for Black to regain the piece.

12 QxPch!!!	KxQ
13 PxB dis ch	K moves
14 N—K7 mate	

QUEEN'S GAMBIT DECLINED

White's mistake: White fails to realize that his 6 P—K3?? is a blunder losing a piece.

Black's refutation: Black sees what White overlooked, and wins the piece.

WHITE	BLACK
1 P—Q4	P—Q4
2 P—QB4	P—QB3
3 N—QB3	N—B3
4 B—N5	N—K5
5 NxN	PxN

At the moment White's advanced Bishop is safe against a possible . . . Q—R4ch, as White has the reply B—Q2 in reserve. However, just to be protected against unpleasant surprises, White would do well to play 6 Q—Q2. Instead:

6 P—K3?? . . .

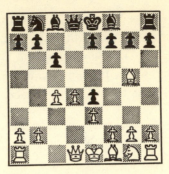

(Position after 6 P—K3??)

With his last move White has cut off the Bishop's retreat, while still leaving that piece exposed to a murderous double attack. Black seizes his chance to win a piece.

6 ... Q—R4ch

White resigns, as he loses his Bishop.

ALBIN COUNTER GAMBIT

White's mistakes: White's 6 B—Q3? is careless, as he overlooks Black's startling reply. His 7 BxB?? is even worse, as the penalty is deadly.

Black's refutation: Black operates with keen surprise moves. He relies on superior tactics.

WHITE	BLACK
1 P—Q4	P—Q4
2 P—QB4	P—K4

106

3 QPxP	P—Q5
4 P—K3	N—QB3
5 P—QR3	B—KB4
6 B—Q3?	. . .

The right way is 6 N—KB3, P—QR4; 7 B—Q3 when the combination later adopted by Black in the game will not work. Why? (See final note.)

| 6 . . . | PxP!! |

(Position after 6 . . . PxP!!)

Black's last move is so unexpected that it ought to put White on his guard. Unfortunately for White, he misses the point.

| 7 BxB?? | PxPch |
| 8 K—K2 | QxQch |

White resigns, for if 9 KxQ, P—B8/Qch. (Observe that if White had developed his King Knight, he would now be able to capture the new Queen.)

SICILIAN DEFENSE

White's mistake: By playing 8 Q—Q5 White mistakenly believes he has extracted *all* the venom from 7 . . . Q—R4!

Black's refutation: By giving up his Queen, Black is able to promote another one, with a decisive gain of material.

WHITE	BLACK
1 P—K4	P—QB4
2 P—QN4	PxP
3 P—Q4	P—K4!
4 PxP	N—QB3
5 N—KB3	KN—K2
6 B—KB4	N—N3
7 B—N3	Q—R4!
8 Q—Q5	P—N6 dis ch

The beauty of Black's last move is that the plausible 9 QxQ?? will *not* do. (9 QN—Q2 is the safest.)

9 QxQ??   . . .

(Position after 9 QxQ??)

White has completely missed the point, but who can blame him? Now Black's diabolical plan unfolds: he has no intention of playing the banal and ineffectual 9 . . . NxQ?

	WHITE	BLACK
9	. . .	P—N7!!
10	Q—B3	B—N5!
11	QxB	NxQ
12	Resigns	

For White cannot prevent 12 . . . PxR/Q!

SICILIAN DEFENSE

Black's mistake: Black's 10 . . . Q—R4 is *potentially* dangerous, as is shown two moves later. His 12 . . . KR—Q1?? leads to immediate disaster.

White's refutation: White loses no time in exploiting the weakness of 12 . . . KR—Q1?? by a neat finesse.

	WHITE	BLACK
1	P—K4	P—QB4
2	N—QB3	N—QB3
3	P—KN3	P—KN3
4	B—N2	B—N2
5	KN—K2	P—Q3
6	P—Q3	N—B3
7	Castles	Castles
8	B—B4	B—Q2

9	Q—Q2	R—K1
10	P—KR3	Q—R4
11	B—R6	B—R1
12	P—B4	KR—Q1??

(Position after 12 . . . KR—Q1??)

For reasons that will at once become clear, Black should have kept his King Rook at King 1 to guard his King Pawn. The thoughtless removal of the Rook gives White his chance for a snappy win.

13	P—K5!!	PxP
14	BxN!	Resigns

Why? For after 14 . . . BxB (or 14 . . . PxB) White plays 15 N—Q5! attacking Black's Queen which is now unprotected. If then 15 . . . QxQ; 16 NxP mate. (This is why Black's King Rook should have remained at King 1.) So Black is lost, as he cannot stop mate and save his Queen at the same time.

RUY LOPEZ

Black's mistakes: Black develops his Queen too early (7 ... Q—B3) and then blunders on the very next move (8 ... BxB? instead of 8 ... PxN!).

White's refutation: White has a brilliant, unforeseen resource which highlights Black's mistake.

WHITE	BLACK
1 P—K4	P—K4
2 N—KB3	N—QB3
3 B—N5	B—B4
4 Castles	P—Q3
5 P—Q4	PxP
6 NxP	B—Q2
7 B—K3	Q—B3
8 NxN!?	BxB?
9 PxB	QxP
10 Q—Q4!	...

(Position after 10 Q—Q4!)

An unexpected but complete answer to Black's triple threat of . . . QxR or . . . QxB or . . . PxN.

White's clever move leaves Black without a good reply. White wins a piece after 10 . . . QxQ?; 11 NxQ or the Exchange after 10 . . . QxB; 11 QxNP etc.

10 . . .	QxB
11 QxNP	QxN
12 QxBPch	K—Q1
13 Q—N7	QxKP
14 QxR	Resigns

White wins more material.

BISHOP'S OPENING

Black's mistakes: Black overreaches himself by trying too hard on his sixth move. Simply 6 . . . PxP would have left him with a good game. After that the attempt to maintain a broad center leads from bad to worse.

White's refutation: White sees the hidden possibilities in combined action by his Queen and Bishop.

WHITE	BLACK
1 P—K4	P—K4
2 B—B4	N—KB3
3 P—Q3	P—B3
4 B—KN5	P—Q4
5 BxN	NPxB

112

6	B—N3	P—KB4
7	Q—B3!	BPxP
8	PxP	B—K3
9	N—K2	Q—R4ch
10	QN—B3	R—N1
11	PxP	B—KN5?

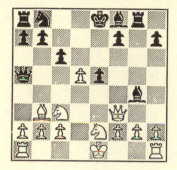

(Position after 11 . . . B—KN5?)

Realizing that he has to lose a Pawn, Black plunges into complications. But White has an astounding sacrifice, based on a powerful discovered check and an unexpected Pawn promotion.

12	QxPch!!	KxQ
13	PxP dis ch	K—N3
14	PxP	B—N5
15	PxR/Q	Q—R3

Threatens . . . QxN mate.

16	Q—K4ch	Resigns

White's material advantage is decisive.

QUEEN'S PAWN OPENING

White's mistakes: White plays the opening too passively (3 P—K3 and 4 QN—Q2) and later on misses Black's threat (12 P—B4! was the right move).

Black's refutation: Black starts a brilliant surprise attack with 12 . . . BxPch! which proves decisive.

	WHITE	BLACK
1	P—Q4	N—KB3
2	N—KB3	P—QN3
3	P—K3	B—N2
4	QN—Q2	P—K3
5	B—Q3	P—Q4
6	Castles	QN—Q2
7	Q—K2	N—K5
8	P—B4	B—Q3
9	N—K1	Castles
10	Q—B3?	P—KB4
11	Q—K2?	R—B3!
12	P—B3?	BxPch!
13	KxB	R—R3ch
14	K—N1	N—N6
15	Q—Q1	Q—R5

Black has built up a winning position. White cannot escape with 16 K—B2 because of 16 . . . N—K5 dbl ch; 17 K—K2, Q—B7ch!; 18 RxQ, N—N6 mate.

(Position after 15 . . . Q—R5)

16 Q—B2   N—R8!

Followed by 17 . . . Q—R7 mate.

5. How to Win by Playing Powerful Moves —

A Do-It-Yourself Quiz with Solutions

In all the games of the previous chapters you have seen how perfectly timed tactics have exacted a severe penalty for faulty play by your opponent. To see these opportunities as they arise on the chessboard, is the very essence of winning quickly. The quiz on the following pages is in the nature of a review. It emphasizes the importance of hitting hard as soon as opportunity arises.

All the positions in this quiz are taken from actual play. In some of these positions the winning process is quite obvious; in others, it is rather subtle. In any case, some decisive action is possible.

So, study each diagram and decide how you would proceed to win forcefully and quickly. Then turn to the solutions to see whether your own solution is the right one. You'll enjoy this quiz, and, above all, it will help you to achieve your purpose—*to beat your opponent quickly.*

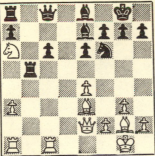

1. White to play and win

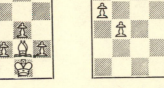

2. White to play and win

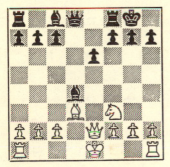

3. White to play and win

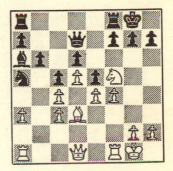

4. White to play and win

(For solutions, see page 136)

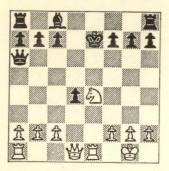

5. White to play and win

6. White to play and win

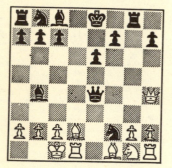

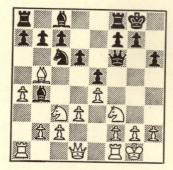

7. White to play and win

8. White to play and win

(For solutions, see pages 136-137)

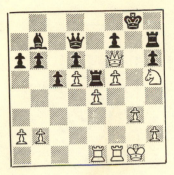

9. White to play and win

10. White to play and win

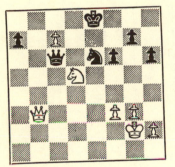

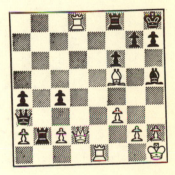

11. White to play and win

12. White to play and win

(For solutions, see pages 137-138)

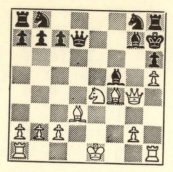

13. White to play and win   14. White to play and win

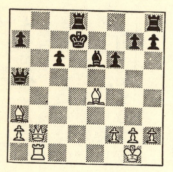

15. White to play and win   16. White to play and win

(For solutions, see pages 138-139)

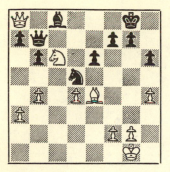 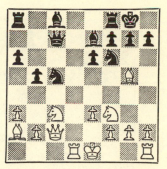

17. White to play and win   18. White to play and win

19. White to play and win   20. White to play and win

(For solutions, see pages 139-140)

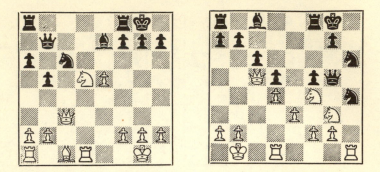

21. White to play and win · 22. White to play and win

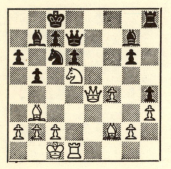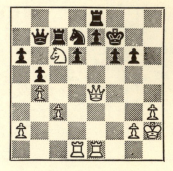

23. White to play and win 24. White to play and win

(For solutions, see pages 140-141)

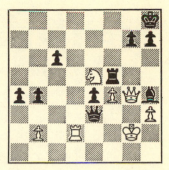

25. White to play and win   26. White to play and win

27. White to play and win   28. White to play and win

(For solutions, see pages 141-142)

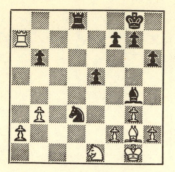 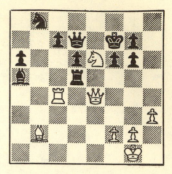

29. White to play and win   30. White to play and win

 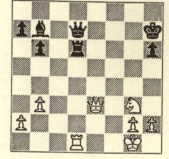

31. White to play and win   32. White to play and win

(For solutions, see pages 143-144)

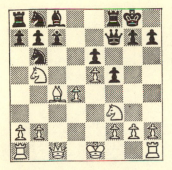

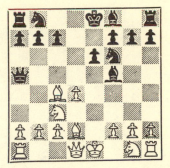

33. White to play and win   34. White to play and win

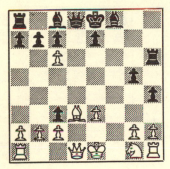

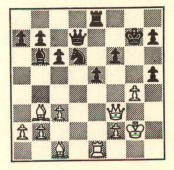

35. White to play and win   36. White to play and win

(For solutions, see pages 144-145)

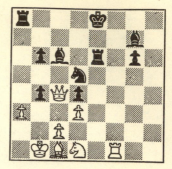

37. White to play and win   38. White to play and win

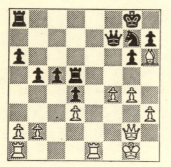

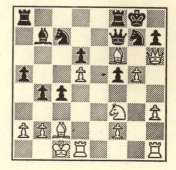

39. White to play and win   40. White to play and win

(For solutions, see pages 145-146)

41. White to play and win

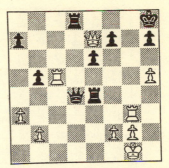

42. White to play and win

43. White to play and win

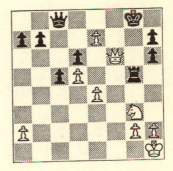

44. White to play and win

(For solutions, see pages 146-147)

45. White to play and win

46. White to play and win

47. White to play and win

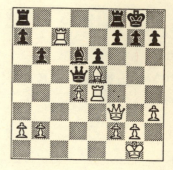

48. White to play and win

(For solutions, see pages 148-149)

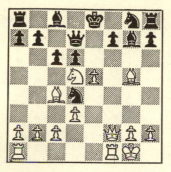

49. White to play and win

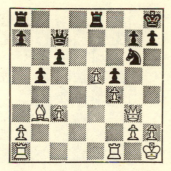

50. White to play and win

51. White to play and win

52. White to play and win

(For solutions, see pages 149-150)

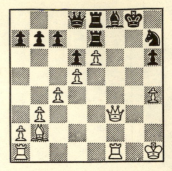

53. White to play and win   54. White to play and win

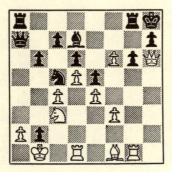

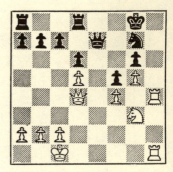

55. White to play and win   56. White to play and win

(For solutions, see pages 150-151)

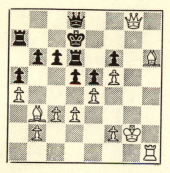
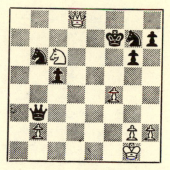

57. White to play and win 58. White to play and win

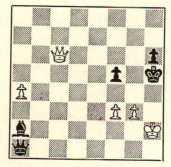
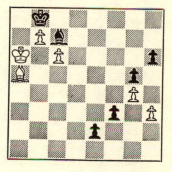

59. White to play and win 60. White to play and win

(For solutions, see pages 151-152)

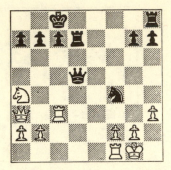

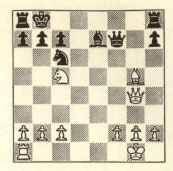

61. White to play and win   62. White to play and win

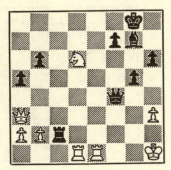

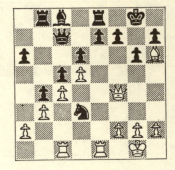

63. White to play and win   64. White to play and win

(For solutions, see pages 152-153)

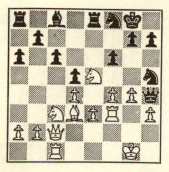 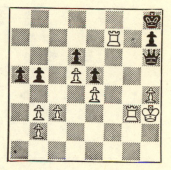

65. White to play and win   66. White to play and win

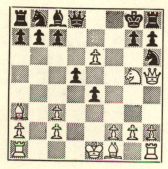 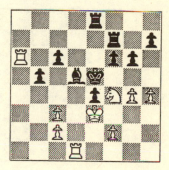

67. White to play and win   68. White to play and win

(For solutions, see pages 153-154)

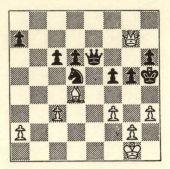

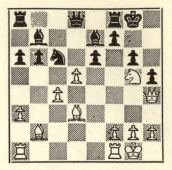

69. White to play and win   70. White to play and win

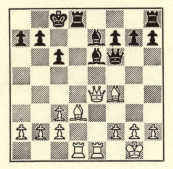

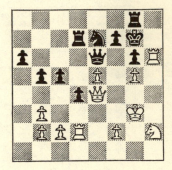

71. White to play and win   72. White to play and win

(For solutions, see pages 154-155)

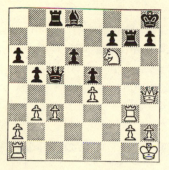

73. White to play and win   74. White to play and win

75. White to play and win   76. White to play and win

(For solutions, see pages 155-156)

SOLUTIONS TO QUIZ

1. White plays 1 N—B7! forking the Black Rooks. If Black replies 1 . . . QxN then White has 2 QxR! winning the Exchange after all, as Black's Queen Bishop Pawn is pinned. (If then 2 . . . PxQ; 3 RxQ and White holds on to his material advantage.)

2. White wins material by a series of sly exchanges ending with a Knight fork:

1 BxB	KxB
2 BxN	KxB
3 N—Q6ch	. . .

Followed, of course, by 4 NxR.

3. White wins by the double attack 1 Q—K4! threatening 2 QxRP mate and also 2 QxB or 2 NxB. Black must stop the mate, whereupon White picks off the Bishop.

4. With 1 Q—N4! White threatens mate next move. Black is forced to play 1 . . . P—N3, whereupon the discovered attack 2 N—R6ch wins the Black Queen.

5. White can give a discovered check by moving his Knight. Which Knight move is the best one? Answer: 1 N—B5 dis ch, which wins the Black Queen.

6. As the situation stands, Black's well-posted Knight prevents the decisive moves 1 R—Q5ch or 1 B—K2ch.

Actually, White *can* play the amazing move 1 R—Q5ch!! Then if Black refuses the Rook, there follows 2 B—B8ch with crushing effect. So Black must capture the Rook, and we get this sequence:

1 R—Q5ch!!	NxR
2 B—K2ch	K—R4
3 R—QR7ch	R—R3
4 RxR mate	

7. White has an amazing forced checkmate, relying on the power of a double check:

1 Q—Q8ch!!	KxQ
2 B—KN5 dbl ch	K—K1
3 R—Q8 mate	

8. White attacks Queen and Bishop with 1 N—Q5! Black replies 1 . . . Q—Q1, whereupon White removes the guardian Knight (2 BxN). After 2 . . . PxB he plays 3 NxB with a piece to the good.

9. If White's Queen were on some other square, he could play 1 N—B6ch winning Black's Queen. So White plays 1 QxR! Then after 1 . . . PxQ he plays 2 N—B6ch and 3 NxQ, winning a Rook by this clearance maneuver.

10. White can win by an exquisite "interference" move: 1 B—Q6!! If Black plays 1 . . . QxQ there follows 2 R—B8 mate. And if 1 . . . RxB; 2 Q—N8ch! forces checkmate.

11. White combines a pin, a Pawn promotion, and a Knight fork in a lovely sequence:

1 Q—N5!!	QxQ
2 P—B8/Qch	K—B2

(If 2 . . . N—Q1; 3 N—B7ch.)

3 QxNch!	KxQ
4 N—B7ch	. . .

Followed by 5 NxQ.

12. Here White takes advantage of the fact that on 1 Q—B3!! Black dare not play 1 . . . QxQ??? because of 2 RxR mate. So we get:

1 Q—B3!!	Q—B4
2 RxRch	QxR
3 QxR and wins	

13. White can win Black's Queen with 1 N—N5ch, PxN; 2 BxBch. However, instead White prefers to give up his own Queen:

1 Q—N6ch!!	BxQ
2 N—N5ch!!	PxN
3 PxB mate	

14. White is a piece down, but he can win the Black Queen by a "skewer" or "X-ray" attack:

1 N—K5ch	K—K3
2 Q—KN8ch	. . .

Followed by 3 QxQ.

15. White takes ruthless advantage of the exposed state of Black's King by playing:

1 BxBPch!!	KxB
2 Q—N7 mate	

16. Who would believe that White has a forced checkmate in two moves? Yet here it is:

1 QxPch!!	PxQ
2 B—QR6 mate	

17. Though Black's position looks secure, it is vulnerable because his Knight and Bishop are pinned. White proves this by:

1 N—K7ch!	QxN

He cannot play 1 . . . NxN?? as his Knight is pinned.

2 QxBch	Q—B1
3 B—R7ch!	. . .

White wins the Queen. White has used a combination of three tactical motifs. His first move is based on a double attack and two pins. His third move "removes the guard."

18. White creates a winning pin by a mating threat:

1 B—N1!	P—N3

The threat was 2 BxN, BxB; 3 QxP mate.

2 BxN	BxB
3 N—K4	B—K2
4 P—QN4!	. . .

The pin enables White to win a piece, as the menaced Knight must not move.

19. Black threatens mate, but White forces the issue with an astounding pin:

1 B—Q4!!	P—K4
2 BxP	QxB
3 Q—R6 mate!	

20. Black's position is constricted but apparently playable. However, when White proceeds with 1 N—N6! he wins Black's Queen, as the King Bishop Pawn is pinned.

21. White convincingly demonstrates the power of a Knight fork:

1 QxN!	QxQ
2 NxBch	K—R1
3 NxQ	. . .

White has won a piece.

22. Here, too, White makes use of a Knight fork to win a piece:

1 RxN!	QxR
2 QxRch!	KxQ
3 N—N6ch	. . .

Followed by 4 NxQ with a piece to the good.

23. A surprising Knight fork leads to a winning pin:

1 N—N6ch!	PxN
2 B—K6	. . .

White wins Black's Queen.

24. White's technique of removing the guard of Black's King Pawn wins the Exchange simply but subtly.

1 N—Q8ch!!	RxN
2 QxKPch	K—N1
3 QxRch	. . .

White wins easily.

25. White maneuvers his Knights cleverly to create a Knight fork that wins the Exchange:

1 N—K7ch	K moves
2 NxP	BxN
3 NxB	. . .

White wins the Exchange by force.

26. Skillful play with the Knight, coupled with Black's weakness on the back rank, tells in White's favor.

1 N—B7ch!!	K—N1

Not 1 . . . RxN; 2 Q—B8ch forcing mate.

2	N—R6ch	K moves
3	QxPch!!	KxQ
4	NxRch	K moves
5	NxQ	. . .

White is a Rook ahead.

27. White wins with a surprising double attack followed by a Knight fork:

1	RxPch!	QxR
2	N—K7ch	. . .

Followed by 3 NxQ.

28. It takes imagination of a high order to see White's third move. Note the "echo" play with the Knight forks.

1	QxN!	RxQ
2	N—B6ch	K—K2
3	NxRch!	K—K1
4	N—B6ch	K—K2
5	NxQ	. . .

White has won the Exchange.

29. Double attack evidently is the real key to White's procedure:

1 NxN	RxN
2 R—R8ch	K—R2
3 B—K4ch	. . .

Followed by 4 BxR with a Rook ahead.

30. White gets nowhere with the plausible 1 QxR because of 1 . . . QxN; 2 QxB, QxR. The right way is:

1 N—Q8ch!	QxN
2 QxRch	K moves
3 QxB	. . .

White is a Rook ahead.

31. White wins by a double attack which is really a "triple attack."

1 P—KB4	B—Q3
2 P—K5	B—B4ch
3 K—R1	N—N1
4 Q—Q5	. . .

Black can resign. White threatens 5 QxBP mate and also QxR and QxB.

32. White's exquisite Queen sacrifice involves a neat pair of alternative double attacks.

| 1 QxRPch!! | KxQ |

Or 1 . . . RxQ; 2 RxQch followed by 3 RxB.

2 RxRch	QxR
3 N—B5ch	K moves
4 NxQ	. . .

White's material advantage of two Pawns is decisive.

33.   White makes clever use of a discovered attack:

| 1 NxBP! | QxN |

In order to save his menaced Rook.

| 2 BxPch | . . . |

White wins the Queen.

34.   Again a discovered attack wins for White—though he also needs to make use of a double attack and a Knight fork.

1 N—Q5!	Q—R5
2 B—QN5ch!	QxB
3 NxPch	. . .

Followed by 4 NxQ.

35.   White neatly demonstrates that Black's King Rook is an overworked piece:

1 Q—R5ch!	RxQ
2 B—N6 mate	

36. White drives Black's Knight into a mating net.

1 B—R6ch!	KxB

On 1 . . . K—N3; 2 PxPch forces the win; or 1 . . . K—R1;
2 QxKBPch etc.

2 QxKBP mate	

37. At the moment, Black has adequate protection for his
critically pinned Knight. But White removes the guard with:

1 R—K8!!	QxR

The alternative is loss of the Queen by 1 . . . NxR; 2 BxQ etc.

2 BxNch	K—N1
3 Q—R8 mate	

38. A remarkable example of removing the guard:

1 R—K1!!	RxR

Or 1 . . . K—Q2; 2 RxR, KxR; 3 QxBch etc.

2 QxBch	. . .

Followed by 3 QxR and wins.

39. Black's Queen guards his Rook at the Queen 4 square. White lashes at the vulnerable Rook with:

1 R—K7! QxR

White has left Black no choice.

2 QxRch . . .

Followed by 3 QxRch and wins.

40. White wins by a remarkably original maneuver:

1 P—N6!! . . .

This leaves Black little choice, for if 1 . . . QxB; 2 QxP mate. Or if 1 . . . PxP; 2 N—N5 and Black must give up his Queen to stop Q—R7 mate.

1 . . . QxNP
2 BxN . . .

Winning at least a piece, for if 2 . . . QxB; 3 R—N1 pins and wins the Black Queen.

41. White's problem is to drive off Black's protective Queen.

1 R—K8ch!! . . .

Clears the sacrificial way for White's Queen.

1 . . . RxR

<pre>
    2 Q—N4ch!!   QxQ
    3 N—B6 mate
</pre>

42. White has a lovely winning move which disturbs the delicate defensive setup that Black has established.

<pre>
    1 R—Q5!!   PxR
</pre>

If 1 . . . RxR; 2 Q—K8 mate or 2 Q—B8 mate. Or 1 . . . QxR; 2 Q—B6 mate.

<pre>
    2 QxRch   . . .
</pre>

White mates next move.

43. White cleverly cuts his opponent's lines of communication.

<pre>
    1 B—B7!!   QxB
</pre>

Or 1 . . . RxB; 2 Q—N7ch!!, RxQ; 3 RxP mate.

<pre>
    2 RxPch!!   QxR
    3 Q—N7ch   KxP
    4 R—R1 mate
</pre>

44. White finds the quickest way:

<pre>
    1 Q—K6ch!   QxQ
    2 PxQ   . . .
</pre>

And there is no way to stop White from queening.

45. Though behind in material, White can win thanks to a promotion trick:

1 R—B8ch!	RxR
2 QxPch!!	KxQ
3 PxR/Nch!	. . .

This promotion to Knight wins the Queen, leaving White with the winning advantage of two Pawns.

46. White spies a microscopic weakness in Black's back rank.

1 RxPch!!	NxR
2 Q—KB7ch	K—N1
3 Q—B8ch!!	RxQ
4 RxR mate	

47. White calmly ignores the attack on his Queen.

1 B—R6!!	R—K1

If 1 . . . RxQ or 1 . . . QxQ; 2 R—B8 mate.

2 PxQ and wins

48. White prepares a subtle Queen sacrifice:

1 R—Q7!	QR—Q1
2 RxB!	RxR
3 Q—B6!!	PxQ

| 4 R—N4ch | K—R1 |
| 5 BxP mate | |

49. White devises a devilish attack against Black's badly exposed King.

| 1 N—B7ch! | QxN |

If 1 . . . K—B1; 2 QxPch, QxQ; 3 RxQ mate.

2 BxPch	K—Q2
3 Q—B5ch!!	NxQ
4 P—K6 mate	

50. White demonstrates the power of a Bishop on a long open diagonal:

| 1 QxN!! | PxQ |

Else he remains a piece down.

| 2 R—B3 | . . . |

Black is helpless against the threat of R—R3 mate.

51. White forces through a magnificent attack against Black's helpless King.

1 Q—Q5!	P—K3
2 QxKP!!	PxQ
3 BxPch	Q—B2
4 RxB!!	QxB
5 R—B8 mate	

52. Black is very weak on the back rank. Therefore:

       1 Q—N5!!   P—N3

If 1 . . . QxQ; 2 RxR mate.

       2 Q—R6!   PxN
       3 R—N4ch!!   PxR
       4 BxPch   K—R1
       5 B—N6 dis ch   K—N1
       6 Q—R7ch   K—B1
       7 QxP mate

53. White has an amazing Queen sacrifice:

       1 QxPch!!   KxQ
       2 PxB dis ch   K—N3
       3 N—K7 mate

54. Here, too, the White Queen is offered to produce an immediate mate.

       1 Q—B7ch!   RxQ
       2 PxR mate

55. Black's Queen is far away. White can sacrifice flamboyantly.

       1 QxRPch!!   KxQ
       2 R—R1ch   B—R6
       3 RxB mate

56.   Black's King seems well protected here, but White smashes the defensive barrier.

1	R—R8ch	K—B2
2	QxNch!!	KxQ
3	R/1—R7 mate	

57.   White wins by an X-ray attack aimed at Black's Rook on Queen Rook 2.

1	Q—R7ch!	Q—K2

Forced.

2	B—B8!	QxQ
3	RxQch	K—K1
4	RxR	KxB

With a piece ahead, White has an easy win.

58.   This time White has an X-ray attack that wins the Black Queen.

1	N—K5ch	K—K3
2	Q—KN8ch	. . .

Followed by 3 QxQ and wins.

59.   Still another X-ray attack. White wins the Black Queen by force.

1	Q—K8ch	K—N4

2 P—B4ch	K—B3

If 2 . . . K—N5; 3 Q—K2 mate.

3 Q—KR8ch	. . .

Followed by 4 QxQ and wins.

60. Blandly ignoring the fact that Black's King Pawn is ready to queen, White forces checkmate:

1 B—N6!!	BxB

If 1 . . . P—K8/Q; 2 B—R7 mate.

2 KxB	any
3 P—B7 mate	

61. Black threatens checkmate. Instead of defending, White replies with a vicious counterattack.

1 N—N6ch!	. . .

This wins Black's Queen, as 1 . . . RPxN allows 2 Q—R8 mate.

62. White forces an artistic smothered mate with the following moves:

1 N—Q7ch	K—B1
2 N—N6 dbl ch	K—N1

If 2 . . . K—Q1; 3 Q—Q7 mate.

3	Q—B8ch!	RxQ
4	N—Q7 mate	

63. Black threatens mate, but White moves first:

1	R—K8ch!	B—B1

If 1 . . . K—R2; 2 Q—Q3ch wins Black's Rook.

2	RxBch!	KxR
3	N—B5 dis ch	K—N1
4	Q—B8ch!!	KxQ
5	R—Q8 mate	

64. Black has set up a triple Knight fork, but White can force checkmate.

1	Q—B6!!	PxQ

Else 2 Q—N7 mate.

2	RxR mate	

65. White exploits the exposed position of Black's Queen.

1	BxKRPch!	NxB

If 1 . . . K—R1; 2 N—B7 mate.

2	N—N6!	. . .

Trapping and winning Black's Queen.

66. White forces the win with a curious move that leaves Black helpless.

1 R—N5!   . . .

Black has no defense. After a few Pawn moves he will be forced to play . . . QxR, leaving him a Rook down.

67. White forces checkmate with an elegant Queen sacrifice:

1 Q—B7ch!   NxQ
2 PxN mate

68. It is hard to believe that with Queens off the board, White could force such a brilliant checkmate:

1 RxBch!   PxR
2 N—Q3ch!   PxN
3 P—B4 mate

69. White's Queen sacrifice leads to an extraordinary mating position.

1 P—N4ch   PxP
2 RPxPch   K—R5
3 QxRPch!!   QxQ
4 K—R2!!   . . .

Followed by 5 B—B2 mate.

70. White's aggressive Bishops are irresistible.

1 QxP!!   . . .

Threatens 2 Q—R7 mate or 2 Q—R8 mate.

1 . . .   PxQ
2 B—R7 mate

71.   White has a Queen sacrifice that tears up Black's castled position by the roots.

1 QxBPch!!   PxQ
2 B—QR6 mate

72.   White has a decisive attack.

1 R—R7ch!!   K—B1

Or 1 . . . KxR; 2 Q—R4ch, K—N2; 3 Q—R6 mate.

2 Q—R8ch   N—B1

Forced.

3 QxNch   . . .

With a piece ahead, White wins easily.

73.   White exploits the awkward defensive position of Black's pieces:

1 QxPch!!   RxQ
2 R—N8 mate

74. Here, too, Black is helpless against White's surprise attack:

1	QxRch!!	KxQ
2	P—K7 mate	

75. Black's broken-up King-side is a welcome target:

1	Q—N4ch	Q—N3

King moves allow 2 Q—N7 mate.

2	N—K7ch	. . .

White wins Black's Queen.

76. Again a brilliant Queen sacrifice is based on the ineffectual position of the Black pieces:

1	QxNch!!	K—N1

If 1 . . . KxQ; 2 B—K5 mate.

2	B—K5	. . .

Black has no defense to the mating threat.

Index